ESSENTIAL OILS

RELAXING AND HEALING

NANDI

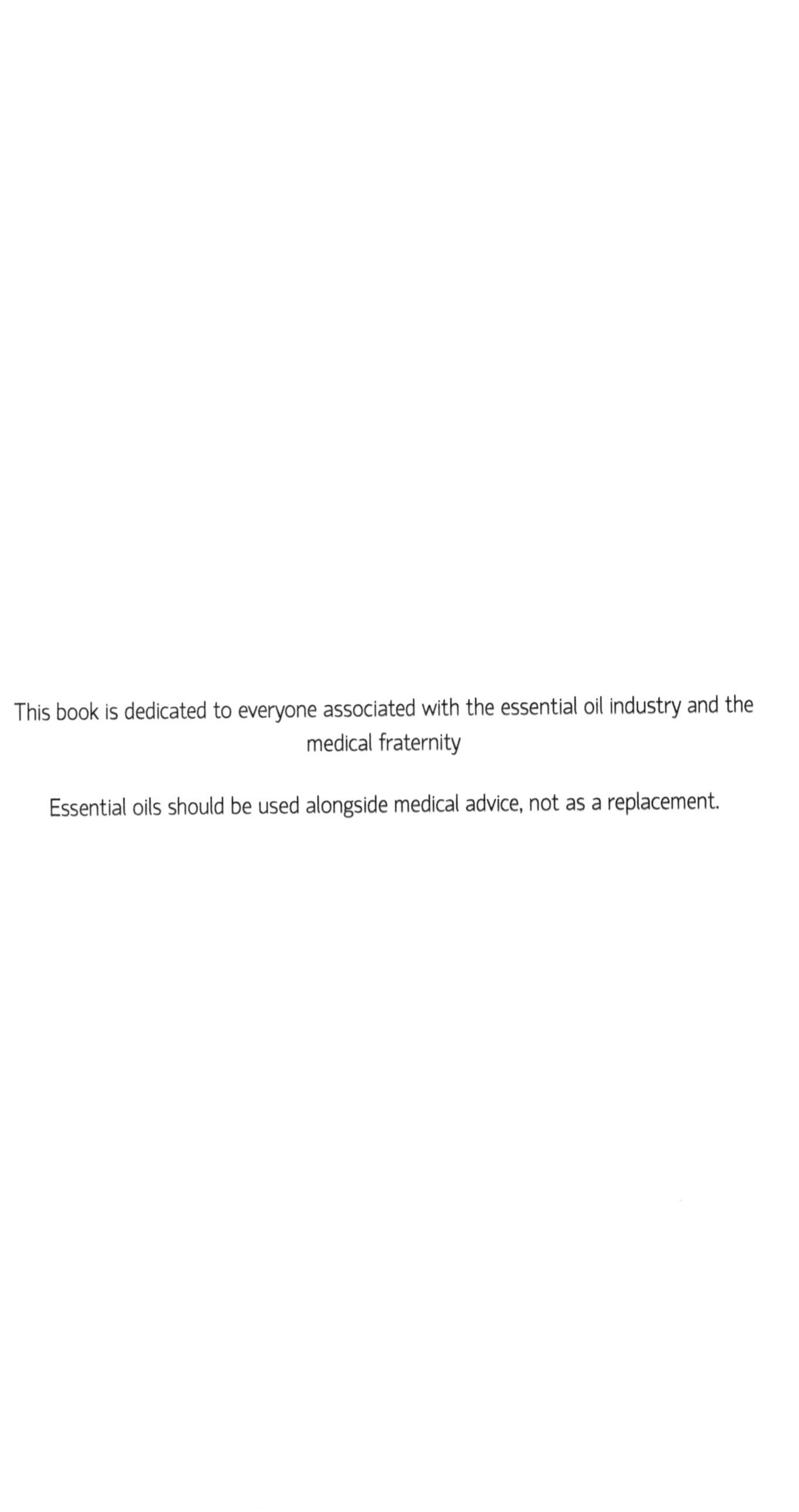

This book is dedicated to everyone associated with the essential oil industry and the medical fraternity

Essential oils should be used alongside medical advice, not as a replacement.

Contents

Contents

Contents

Contents

Foreword

Essential oils, the concentrated essences extracted from plants, have captivated humanity for centuries. Today, they continue to offer a natural approach to enhancing our well-being.

This book provides a clear and accessible introduction to the wonders of essential oils, highlighting their safe and effective use. This could be a good book for a curious beginner.

Preface

Welcome to the fascinating world of essential oils! This book is your comprehensive guide, written specifically for beginners. Here, we explore the history, science, and practical applications of these potent plant extracts. How to safey and effective use essential oils and encouraging you to integrate them seamlessly into your daily routine for improved well-being. This guide is your stepping stone to explore the world of essential oils.

Acknowledgements

Books:

"Complete Guide to Essential Oils & Aromatherapy" by Valerie Ann Worwood

"The Complete Book of Essential Oils and Aromatherapy" by Valerie Warner (a great reference book for beginners)

"Alchemy of Herbs" by Patricia Sanchez (focuses on the history and folklore of essential oils)

"Essential Oils for Everyone" by Valerie Ann Worwood (practical guide to using essential oils for everyday ailments)

Baser, K.H.C., G. Buchbauer (2010). Handbook of Essential Oils: Science, Technology and Applications. CRC Press, Boca Raton, London, New York. ISBN 978-1-4200-6315-8.

Schnaubelt, Kurt (1999). Advanced Aromatherapy: The Science of Essential Oil Therapy. Healing Arts Press. ISBN 978-0-89281-743-6.

Sellar, Wanda (2001). The Directory of Essential Oils (Reprint ed.). Essex: The C.W. Daniel Company, Ltd. ISBN 978-0-85207-346-9.

Tisserand, Robert (1995). Essential Oil Safety: A Guide for Health Care Professionals. Churchill Livingstone. ISBN 978-0-443-05260-6.

Rimal V, Shishodia S, Srivastava PK, Gupta S, Mallick AI (2021). "Synthesis and characterization of Indian essential oil Carbon Dots for interdisciplinary application.

Robert Tisserand: Another prominent figure in the field, Tisserand is known for his scientific approach to essential oils.

Speakers:

Dr. Robert Pappas: A clinical aromatherapist and researcher, Dr. Pappas lectures on the science and safe use of essential oils. You can find videos of his lectures online.

Lydia Rachael: An aromatherapist and educator, Rachael offers online courses and workshops on essential oil use.

Andrea Butner: An aromatherapist and author, Butner frequently speaks at conferences and events on essential oils.

Organizations:

National Association for Holistic Aromatherapy (NAHA): A UK-based organization that promotes the safe and effective use of essential oils. https://naha.org/

Alliance Internationale des Aromathérapeutes (ALIA): An international organization that sets standards for aromatherapy education and practice. https://www.alliance-aromatherapists.org/Aromatherapy

American College of Healthcare Aromatherapy (ACHHA): A US-based organization that provides education and certification for aromatherapists. https://www.nccih.nih.gov/health/aromatherapy

wikipedia

Chatgpt

Gemini

Prologue

Congratulations! You've just started your essential oil exploration. Don't hesitate to consult with qualified aromatherapists or healthcare professionals for personalized guidance. The world of essential oils offers endless possibilities.

CHAPTER ONE

HISTORY OF ESSENTIAL OILS

The captivating world of essential oils boasts a rich and fascinating history, stretching back millennia. From their earliest uses in ancient civilizations to their modern-day applications in aromatherapy, essential oils have consistently played a significant role in human culture.

Early Civilizations (4,000 BC and Beyond): Evidence suggests some of the earliest uses of aromatic plants and resins date back to prehistoric times. Analysis of pollen found near Stone Age settlements hints at the use of aromatic plants for medicinal purposes.

Egypt (3,000 BC Onwards): The Egyptians were pioneers in utilizing essential oils for religious ceremonies, embalming practices, and cosmetic applications. They extracted oils from plants like frankincense, myrrh, and cedarwood, using them in elaborate rituals and beauty treatments.

China and India (2,500 BC Onwards): Traditional Chinese Medicine and Ayurveda, the ancient Indian medical system, both incorporated aromatic plants and essential oils into their healing practices. They believed these oils possessed therapeutic properties and used them for massage, inhalation, and internal consumption.

The Greco-Roman World (1,500 BC Onwards): The Greeks and Romans adopted the knowledge of essential oils from the Egyptians. They used them for medicinal purposes, cosmetics, and even in warfare. The famous physician Hippocrates advocated for the use of pleasant-smelling plants for healing.

The Islamic Golden Age (8th-13th Centuries AD): Islamic scholars played a pivotal role in advancing the knowledge of essential oils. They developed and refined distillation techniques, a process that revolutionized essential oil extraction, making it more efficient. The Persian physician Ibn Sina (known as Avicenna in the West) documented the uses of various essential oils in his medical texts.

Europe in the Middle Ages (11ᵗʰ-15ᵗʰ Centuries AD): The knowledge of distillation spread to Europe during the Middle Ages. Essential oils became a staple in European pharmacies and were used for a variety of ailments. Distilled products like rosewater, lavender oil, and rosemary oil gained popularity.

19ᵗʰ Century: The 19ᵗʰ century saw a renewed interest in essential oils, particularly in France. The city of Grasse became a center for perfume production, and the study of essential oils gained momentum.

20ᵗʰ Century and Beyond: The 20ᵗʰ century witnessed the birth of modern aromatherapy. French chemist René-Maurice Gattefossé coined the term "aromatherapy" in the 1930s after experiencing the healing properties of lavender oil on a burn.

Today, essential oils are popular and extensively used for beauty and wellness.

CHAPTER TWO

ESSENTIAL OILS AND RELIGIONS

Holy books of different religions have mentioned many fragrant plants and oils, though the term "essential oil" itself isn't used.

Essential Oils in the Bible: The use of aromatic substances mentioned in the Bible is often associated with their fragrance, symbolism, and spiritual significance.

- Frankincense and Myrrh were highly valued for their fragrance and were used in religious rituals, anointing practices, and as offerings.
- Spikenard symbolizing an act of love and devotion.
- Cassia and Cinnamon were associated with purification, consecration, and divine favor.
- Hyssop is an aromatic herb mentioned in the Bible for its purifying properties.
- Myrtle is mentioned in the Bible as a symbol of beauty, joy, and abundance.

Essential Oils in Islam: The use of aromatic substances in Islam is often associated with spirituality, purification, and enhancing one's connection to the divine.

- Oudh is mentioned in Islamic poetry and literature as a symbol of luxury, purity, and spiritual enlightenment.
- Frankincense and Myrrh were offered as gifts and used in religious practices for their pleasing fragrance and perceived spiritual significance.
- Camphor is mentioned in the Quran for its fragrance and cooling properties.

- Rose Water is widely used in Islamic cultures for its fragrance and as a symbol of purity and beauty.
- Black Seed Oil (Nigella Sativa)is used in Islamic medicine for various ailments, including respiratory conditions, digestive issues, and skin problems.
- Sandalwood and Musk are also mentioned in Islamic literature for their fragrance.

Essential Oils in Buddhism: The use of aromatic substances in Buddhism reflects the tradition's emphasis on mindfulness, inner peace, and reverence for the natural world.

- Sandalwood is valued for its calming fragrance and is believed to aid in meditation and spiritual practices.
- Lotus flower is highly revered in Buddhism as a symbol of purity, enlightenment, and spiritual awakening.
- Frankincense and Myrrh is used in Buddhist rituals and ceremonies for their pleasant fragrance and symbolic significance.
- Camphor is burned as incense to purify the air and create a sacred atmosphere.
- Cedarwood is used in Buddhist practices for its grounding and calming properties. Often diffused during meditation sessions to promote a sense of inner peace and tranquility.

Essential Oils in Hinduism: The use of aromatic substances in Hindu rituals and ceremonies reflects the tradition's emphasis on reverence for nature, purification, and spiritual enlightenment.

- Sandalwood is highly valued for its soothing fragrance and cooling properties.
- Tulsi (Holy Basil) is believed to have purifying properties and is used to cleanse the mind, body, and spirit.
- Patchouli is used to create a sacred atmosphere.
- Jasmine is revered for its sweet and floral fragrance and is often used in Hindu weddings, festivals, and ceremonies as a symbol of purity, love, and devotion. It is also associated with the Hindu goddess Lakshmi, the goddess of wealth and prosperity.

- Rose is used in Hindu rituals and ceremonies for its uplifting and heart-opening properties.
- Camphor is burned as incense during puja and arati (ritual of waving lighted lamps) to purify the environment and create a sacred atmosphere.

Essential Oils in Egypt: Essential oils held immense cultural, religious, and practical significance in ancient Egypt. Egyptians were one of the first cultures to use essential oils extensively.

- Peppermint, Eucalyptus, and Thyme were utilized for their medicinal properties.
- Cedarwood, Myrrh, and Frankincense were used in embalming techniques to prevent decomposition and to impart a pleasant scent to the mummified remains.
- Rosemary, Lavender, and Almond were used in cosmetics, perfumes, and hair care products.
- Lavender, Chamomile, and Sandalwood were used in aromatherapy to alleviate stress, anxiety, and insomnia.

CHAPTER THREE

UNDERSTANDING ESSENTIAL OILS

Essential oils, often referred to as volatile oils or ethereal oils, are concentrated liquid extracts captured from various parts of aromatic plants – flowers, leaves, seeds, bark, and roots. These potent liquids hold the very essence of the plant, capturing its fragrance and a multitude of beneficial properties. Unlike carrier oils, which are vegetable oils extracted through pressing (e.g., almond oil, coconut oil), essential oils are much more concentrated and require dilution before topical application.

Essential oils are a complex blend of hundreds of volatile aromatic compounds. These constituents, primarily terpenes and phenolics, are responsible for the unique scent and therapeutic properties of each oil.

Terpenes: These are the most abundant constituents in essential oils. They contribute significantly to the aroma and offer various therapeutic benefits, including promoting relaxation, reducing inflammation, and even supporting the immune system. Examples of terpenes include limonene (found in citrus peels) and linalool (found in lavender).

Phenolics: This class of compounds includes well-known antioxidants like thymol (found in thyme oil) and eugenol (found in clove oil). They contribute to the spicy or antiseptic properties of some essential oils.

Several methods are used to extract essential oils from plants, each with its own advantages and limitations.

The most common methods include:

Steam Distillation: This is the most widely used method. Plant material is placed in a still, and steam is passed through it. The steam carries the volatile oil molecules, which are then cooled, condensed and collected.

Cold Pressing: This method is primarily used for citrus fruits. The rinds are pressed to release the essential oil without the use of heat.

Solvent Extraction: This method uses solvents to extract the essential oils. It is less common due to potential concerns about residual solvents in the final product.

When selecting essential oils, quality matters. Look for oils that are:

100% Pure and Natural: Free from additives, fillers, or synthetic fragrances.

Essential oils are potent and should be used with care. Here are some key safety precautions to remember:

Dilution is important: Essential oils are highly concentrated and must be diluted with a carrier oil like jojoba, almond, or coconut oil before applying them to your skin. A common ratio is 2-3 drops of essential oil per 1 tablespoon of carrier oil.

Sensitivity: Always do a patch test before using a new essential oil. Apply a small amount of the diluted blend to your inner forearm and wait 24 hours to see if there's any irritation.

Sun Sensitivity: Some essential oils like citrus oils (lemon, grapefruit) can increase sun sensitivity. Avoid using them on exposed skin if you have to go out in the Sun.

Less is More: Start with a small amount of essential oil and gradually increase as needed.

Sensitive Areas: Avoid contact with eyes, mucous membranes, and damaged skin.

Pregnancy and Children: Consult a healthcare professional before using essential oils if pregnant, breastfeeding, or using them on children(below 9 years).

Remember: Consistency is key! Regularly using essential oil blends tailored to your skin type can offer noticeable benefits.

Essential oils should be used alongside medical advice, not as a replacement.

CHAPTER FOUR

CHEMICAL CONSTITUENTS OF ESSENTIAL OILS

Essential oils are complex mixtures of volatile compounds produced by aromatic plants. These volatile compounds are what give essential oils their characteristic aromas and flavors. The chemical constituents of essential oils can be broadly classified into two main groups: terpenoids and non-terpenoids.

Terpenoids: These are the most common constituents of essential oils, typically making up 80% or more of the oil's composition. Terpenoids are a large and diverse class of organic compounds that are synthesized from the five-carbon molecule isoprene. There are two main types of terpenoids found in essential oils: monoterpenes and sesquiterpenes.

Monoterpenes:These are smaller terpenoids with 10 carbon atoms. Some common monoterpenes found in essential oils include limonene (found in citrus peels), linalool (found in lavender), and alpha-pinene (found in pine needles).

Sesquiterpenes:These are larger terpenoids with 15 carbon atoms. Some common sesquiterpenes found in essential oils include beta-caryophyllene (found in cloves) and germacrene D (found in chamomile).

Non-terpenoids:These are a smaller group of compounds that make up the remaining 20% or less of an essential oil's composition. Some common non-terpenoids found in essential oils include alcohols (such as menthol in peppermint), aldehydes (such as citral in lemongrass), and esters (such as geranyl acetate in rose).

The specific chemical constituents of an essential oil can vary depending on a number of factors, including the plant species, the part of the plant from which the oil is extracted, the climate and soil conditions in which the plant is grown, and the extraction method used. The chemical composition of an essential oil is what determines its therapeutic properties. For example, lavender oil is known for its calming and relaxing effects, which is due in part to its high concentration of linalool.

It's important to note that essential oils are concentrated and can be irritating to the skin and mucous membranes. Always dilute essential oils in a carrier oil, such as almond oil or jojoba oil, before using them topically. Essential oils should also not be ingested, as they can be toxic.

ESSENTIAL OIL PRECAUTIONS AND SAFE PRACTICES

Essential oils, while boasting a multitude of benefits, are potent and require responsible use.

Unlike carrier oils (such as almond or coconut oil) meant for direct application, essential oils are highly concentrated and can irritate the skin upon direct contact.

Dilution is necessary when using essential oils topically for the following reasons.

Preserves Skin Integrity: Undiluted essential oils can strip away the skin's natural oils, leading to dryness, redness, and even burns. Dilution with a carrier oil creates a safer and gentler application.

Optimizes Absorption: Diluted essential oils penetrate the skin more effectively, allowing for better absorption.

Common carrier oils include sweet almond oil, jojoba oil, grapeseed oil, and coconut oil. Each offers a slightly different texture and absorption rate.

Dry Skin: choose a richer carrier oil like avocado oil or apricot kernel oil.

Oily Skin: choose a lighter carrier oils like grapeseed oil or jojoba oil.

The recommended dilution ratio for topical application typically falls between 1-5%. Here's a breakdown:

1% Dilution: Ideal for sensitive skin or children. Use 1 drop of essential oil to 1 tablespoon (15 ml) of carrier oil.

2-3% Dilution: for adults. Use 2-3 drops of essential oil to 1 tablespoon of carrier oil.

5% Dilution: Suitable for experienced users or localized areas like muscle aches. Use no more than 5 drops of essential oil to 1 tablespoon of carrier oil.

Always perform a patch test before full application. Apply a diluted amount of the essential oil blend to a small area of your inner forearm and wait 24 hours to monitor for any irritation.

Sun Sensitivity: Some essential oils (e.g., citrus oils) can increase sun sensitivity. Avoid sun exposure for at least 12 hours after topical application of these oils.

Pregnancy and Children: Consult a healthcare professional before using essential oils if pregnant, breastfeeding, or using them on children.

Internal Use: Avoid ingesting essential oils unless under the guidance of a qualified aromatherapist or healthcare professional.

Eyes and Mucous Membranes: Essential oils should never come in contact with eyes or mucous membranes (nose, mouth, genitals).

Fire Hazard: Essential oils are flammable. Keep them away from open flames and heat sources.

Always store essential oils in dark, cool glass containers. Light and heat can degrade the quality of essential oils.

Keep essential oils out of reach of children and pets.

Tightly secure lids after each use. This prevents evaporation and maintains the potency of the oil.

CHAPTER SIX

VERSATILE ESSENTIAL OILS

Lavender (Lavandula angustifolia): Renowned for its calming and relaxing aroma.

Benefits: Promotes relaxation, reduces stress and anxiety, improves sleep quality, soothes minor skin irritations.

Uses: Diffuse for a calming atmosphere, apply diluted topically for relaxation or on minor burns and insect bites (after patch test).

Tea Tree (Melaleuca alternifolia): Celebrated for its purifying and cleansing properties, tea tree oil is a natural choice for skin concerns.

Benefits: Promotes healthy skin, combats blemishes, soothes minor cuts and scrapes, possesses antibacterial and antifungal properties.

Uses: Dilute for topical application on blemishes, add a drop to a natural cleaning solution.

Peppermint (Mentha piperita): Known for its invigorating aroma and cooling sensation, peppermint oil makes you feel fresh.

Benefits: Improves focus and alertness, relieves headaches, eases nausea, promotes healthy digestion.

Uses: Diffuse for an energy boost, inhale for nausea relief, apply diluted topically on temples for headaches (after patch test).

Lemon (Citrus): Bursting with a bright and uplifting aroma, lemon oil offers a refreshing and cleansing experience.

Benefits: Uplifts mood and promotes mental clarity, supports healthy digestion, possesses natural cleansing properties.

Uses: Diffuse for a mood boost, add a drop to a homemade cleaning solution (diluted) for a refreshing scent.

Eucalyptus (Eucalyptus globulus): Renowned for its energizing aroma and respiratory benefits.

Benefits: Clears congestion, promotes easier breathing, relieves muscle aches and pains.

Uses: Diffuse for respiratory support, apply diluted topically to achy muscles (after patch test).

SELECTING QUALITY ESSENTIAL OILS

Purity and Potency: High-quality oils are 100% pure, free from adulterants, fillers, or synthetic fragrances. This ensures you receive the genuine therapeutic benefits of the plant.

Safety: Adulterated or low-quality essential oils may contain harmful chemicals that can irritate the skin or pose health risks.

Aroma: Pure essential oils possess a true and complex aroma, reflecting the essence of the plant.

Processing Method: Steam distillation is generally considered the preferred method for extracting high-quality essential oils.

Plant Part Used: Different parts of the plant (flowers, leaves, etc.) can yield essential oils with slightly varying properties.

Price: Quality essential oil is not cheap.

CHAPTER EIGHT

AROMATHERAPY

René-Maurice Gattefossé, was a French chemist who lived in the early 20th century. He's credited with coining the term "aromatherapy" and laying the groundwork for the modern study of essential oils. His book "Aromathérapie" published in 1937 helped establish aromatherapy.

The Art of Aromatherapy:

Aromatherapy, the practice of using essential oils for therapeutic purposes, offers a holistic approach to well-being. By harnessing the power of scent, aromatherapy can promote relaxation, improve mood, alleviate discomfort, and enhance overall health.

The Science of Scent: Our sense of smell plays a powerful role in influencing our emotions and physical state. When we inhale essential oil molecules, they travel up the olfactory nerve to the limbic system, the part of the brain responsible for emotions, memory, and hormone regulation. These aromatic compounds can trigger various physiological responses, leading to the therapeutic benefits associated with aromatherapy.

Methods of Aromatherapy:

Inhalation: This is the most common method. You can inhale essential oils directly from the bottle, use a diffuser to disperse them into the air, or add a few drops to a steaming bowl of water for a facial steam.

Topical Application: Essential oils must be diluted in a carrier oil before topical application to avoid skin irritation. Once diluted, they can be massaged into the skin, applied to specific areas like temples or the soles of the feet, or used in compresses.

Bathing: Adding a few drops of diluted essential oil to your bathwater can create a relaxing and therapeutic bathing experience.

Diffusers: Diffusers come in various styles, using water or heat to disperse essential oils into the air. This method allows you to subtly fill a room with a specific aroma.

Choosing the Right Method:

The best method for you depends on your desired outcome and personal preference.

For relaxation and mood enhancement: Diffusion or inhalation are great options.

For targeted relief of muscle aches or pain: Topical application with dilution is ideal.

For creating a calming bath ritual: Adding diluted essential oils to your bathwater can be very soothing.

Safety Considerations in Aromatherapy:

Always prioritize safety when using essential oils for aromatherapy:

Essential oils must be diluted in a carrier oil before topical application.

Start with a small amount of essential oil and gradually increase as needed.

Avoid contact with eyes, mucous membranes, and broken skin.

Consult a healthcare professional before using essential oils if pregnant, breastfeeding, or using them on children. Certain essential oils are not recommended during pregnancy or for young children.

Building Your Aromatherapy Routine:

What do you hope to achieve with aromatherapy? Relaxation, focus, or improved sleep?

Select oils based on your desired outcome and personal preference for aroma.

Experiment with inhalation, diffusion, and topical application (with dilution) to find what works best for you.

Begin with a low dilution and gradually increase as needed to assess your tolerance.

Creating a Relaxing Aromatherapy Ritual:

Dim the lights and create a calming atmosphere.

Light a candle or diffuse a relaxing essential oil blend (lavender, chamomile).

Calming music in the background.

Close your eyes and take slow, deep breaths, inhaling the aromatic blend.

Focus on releasing tension and let go.

Let the aromatherapy magic unfold.

CHAPTER NINE

CRAFTING YOUR OWN ESSENTIAL OIL BLENDS

The world of essential oils offers a vast array of aromas and therapeutic benefits. By venturing beyond single oils and creating your own custom blends, you can personalize your aromatherapy experience to address specific needs.

The Art of Blending:

Synergy is the key concept in essential oil blending. When you combine different essential oils, their therapeutic properties can work together in a harmonious way, often creating a more potent effect than using a single oil alone. Consider these factors when crafting your blends:

Top Note: These essential oils have a light, refreshing aroma and evaporate quickly. Examples include citrus oils (lemon, orange) and peppermint.

Middle Note: These form the heart of the blend, offering a balancing and grounding effect. Examples include lavender, chamomile, and clary sage.

Base Note: These essential oils have a heavier aroma and evaporate slowly, providing depth and anchoring to the blend. Examples include sandalwood, vetiver, and cedarwood.

Building a Blend:

- What are you hoping to achieve with your blend? Relaxation, stress relief, improved sleep, or respiratory support?
- Select essential oils known for their properties that align with your desired outcome.
- Choose oils that complement each other aromatically. Experiment by smelling individual oils and then together to create a pleasing blend.
- For beginners, it's best to start with 2-3 essential oils. As you gain experience, you can create more complex blends.

Dilution is Key: Remember to always dilute your essential oil blend in a carrier oil before use. Always dilute essential oils before topical application. Refer to Chapter 3 for dilution ratios and essential oil safety precautions.

Essential Oil Blend Recipes to Get You Started:

Relaxation Blend: 3 drops lavender, 2 drops chamomile, 1 drop sandalwood.

Focus Blend: 3 drops peppermint, 2 drops rosemary, 1 drop lemon.

Sleep Blend: 4 drops lavender, 3 drops Roman chamomile, 2 drops vetiver.

Start with a small amount of the blend and test it on a small area of your skin.

The beauty of DIY essential oil blending lies in its personalization. Don't be afraid to experiment with different combinations and ratios to discover blends that perfectly suit your needs and preferences. With practice and exploration, you'll gain confidence.

CHAPTER TEN

ESSENTIAL OILS FOR EVERYDAY WELLNESS

Essential oils offer a natural and complementary approach to self-care, promoting well-being and addressing various common concerns.

Essential Oils for Stress and Anxiety:

Lavender: Renowned for its calming properties, lavender oil can promote relaxation and ease feelings of tension.

Bergamot: Uplifting and mood-balancing, bergamot oil can help reduce anxiety and create a sense of calm. inhale directly or diffuse it for a mood boost.

Chamomile: Known for its calming and soothing properties, chamomile oil can ease anxious feelings and promote relaxation.

Essential Oils for Enhancing Sleep Quality:

Lavender: Diffuse it in your bedroom or add a few drops to your pillowcase to create a calming sleep environment.

Vetiver: Grounding and calming, vetiver oil can ease restlessness and promote deeper sleep.

Cedarwood: Known for its relaxing and sleep-promoting properties, cedarwood oil can create a sense of peace and tranquility. Diffuse it or add a drop to your pillowcase (diluted) to promote restful sleep.

Essential Oils for Relief from Common Aches and Pains:

Peppermint: Known for its analgesic properties, peppermint oil can help relieve muscle aches and headaches.

Eucalyptus: With its anti-inflammatory properties, eucalyptus oil can ease muscle tension and joint pain.

Clary Sage: Known for its muscle-relaxing properties, clary sage oil can help alleviate menstrual cramps and headaches.

Essential Oils for Respiratory Issues:

Tea Tree: With its cleansing properties, tea tree oil can help clear congestion and ease coughs.

Eucalyptus: Known for its expectorant properties, eucalyptus oil can help clear mucus and ease congestion.

Lemon: Refreshing and cleansing, lemon oil can help ease congestion and promote clear breathing.

Creative Applications of Essential Oils:

Natural Cleaning Solutions: Certain essential oils, like lemon and tea tree oil (diluted!), can be incorporated into homemade cleaning solutions for a fresh and natural approach.

Freshen Up Your Laundry: Add a few drops of your favorite essential oil (diluted in water) to a dryer ball for a touch of fragrance on your laundry (avoid using oils that can stain).

Deodorize Your Car: Diffuse a refreshing essential oil blend (like citrus or peppermint) to eliminate lingering odors in your car.

Caution:

- Always dilute essential oils before topical application.
- Consult a healthcare professional before using essential oils if pregnant, breastfeeding, or using them on children.
- Certain essential oils may have contraindications, so research individual oils before use.

Essential oils offer a fragrant and versatile approach to enhancing your everyday well-being.

CHAPTER ELEVEN

EMERGING APPLICATION OF ESSENTIAL OILS

Essential Oils in Medicine and Wellness:

Aromatherapy Research: Clinical research is increasingly exploring the therapeutic benefits of essential oils for anxiety, depression, pain management, and even sleep disorders.

Microbial Applications: Certain essential oils exhibit antimicrobial and antifungal properties. Research is ongoing to explore their potential use as natural disinfectants and for combating antibiotic-resistant bacteria.

Essential Oils in Food and Beverage Industry:

Flavor Enhancements: Specific essential oils, like citrus extracts or peppermint oil, can be used to enhance the flavor profile of food and beverages without resorting to artificial additives.

Food Preservation: Some essential oils like spice oils, possess natural preservative properties, offering a potential alternative to synthetic preservatives in the food industry.

Essential Oils in Agriculture:

Pest Control: Certain essential oils, like neem oil or clove oil, have shown promise as natural pest repellents, offering a more sustainable approach to pest management in agriculture.

Plant Growth Promoters: Research suggests some essential oils can stimulate plant growth and enhance their resistance to disease. This could lead to the development of natural alternatives to synthetic fertilizers and pesticides.

Advanced Delivery Systems:

Nanoparticles: Encapsulating essential oils in nanoparticles may improve their absorption and delivery within the body, potentially leading to more targeted therapeutic applications.

Transdermal Delivery Systems: Novel methods of applying essential oils through skin patches or other transdermal delivery systems could offer sustained and controlled release of their beneficial properties.

CHAPTER TWELVE

METHODS OF USING ESSENTIAL OILS

Aromatic Toweling: after washing as usual, add 2-3 drops of your favorite essential oil on a wet face cloth or sponge; run it briskly all over your body.

Aromatic Baths: sprinkle 4-8 drops of essential oil on to the water's surface after the bath has been drawn.Agitate the water to disperse the oil. The effect of such baths is to reduce tension in body and mind.

Atomisers: use a garden mist pump or a spray bottle to disperse the molecules (dilute in water or rose water or alcohol for best results) into the air in a fine mist.

Compress: add about 6 drops of essential oil to a bowl containing about 500 ml of water, as hot as you can comfortably bear. Place a small towel on top of the water. Wring out the excess and place the towel over the area to be treated or run the towel all over your body. A compress is a valuable way of treating muscular pain, sprains and bruises as well as reducing pain and congestion in internal organs.

Cotton Ball: Add a few drops of essential oil onto cotton ball in a small bowl, and let it slowly disperse the essential oil into the air; this is suitable for wardrobes, office desks and automobiles.

Cream and Shampoo: to enhance the therapeutic effect of your favorite cream or shampoo add a drop of suitable essential oil and feel the difference.

Diffuser: To get the most from your essential oils a diffuser is used to help disperse the molecules into the air. This enables the body to use them as you breathe in the wonderful aromas. Some use electricity and others a heating element or small lit candle under a bowl of water. In the bowl add water and a few drops of your favorite essential oil, the heat generated from the electricity or heating element or a lit candle will warm the water and help disperse the oil molecules into the air.

Foot and Hand Baths: sprinkle 5-6 drops of the appropriate essential oil in a bowl of lukewarm water. Soak feet or hands for about 10 minutes. At the end of a tiring day this can be relaxing and can even alleviate tension headaches.

Gargles and Mouthwashes: for sore throats and laryngitis add one drop of lemon or peppermint oil to a glass containing 2 teaspoonfuls of cider vinegar. Stir well to disperse the oil, and then fill the glass with warm water. Natural essential oil dissolves better in cedar vinegar and also vinegar helps reduce the build-up of tartar on the inside of teeth back.

Inhalations: to help clear nasal passages when you have a cold or flu, put 5-10 drops of essential oil on your handkerchief and inhale as required. Essential oil can also be sprinkled on your pillow to ease nasal congestion and to aid restful sleep.

Neat Application: provided the skin is cooled first under cold running water for at least 5 minutes, lavender, eucalyptus, tea tree or geranium can be applied neat to minor burns and scalds.

Steam Inhalations: pour 500 ml of near boiling water into a bowl and then add 2-4 drops of essential oil. Inhale the vapors for 5-10 minutes. In order to trap the aromatic steam more effectively, drape a towel over your head and the bowl. Steam inhalation helps relieve respiratory problems.

CHAPTER THIRTEEN

ACTION OF ESSENTIAL OILS

Adrenal Stimulants: For stress related exhaustion, for example basil, geranium, rosemary.

Anti–rheumatics: For preventing and relieving rheumatic problems, for example angelica, coriander and juniper.

Antibiotics and bactericidal: Forfighting bacterial infection, for examples lavender, lemongrass, rosemary, teatree.

Antidepressants: For uplifting the spirits, for example bergamot, geranium, lemon, orange, rosemary, ylang ylang.

Anti-diabetics or Hypoglycemic: For helping to balance blood-sugar levels, for example geranium, juniper berry.

Anti-inflammatories: To reduce pain and inflammation in arthritic joints, such essences also help reduce swelling around injuries for example chamomile, galbanum, lavender.

Anti-Inflammatory: Helpful for skin rashes and wounds, for example chamomile, lavender, geranium.

Antiseptic: All essential oils are antiseptic to a greater or lesser degree, though good examples include eucalyptus, lavender, teatree.

Antispasmodics: For preventing and easing menstrual pain and for easing labour, for example chamomile, clary sage, lavender, marjoram, rose otto and for easing spasm, use chamomile, fennel, peppermint.

Antivirals: For protecting against and helping to reduce serious complications of viral infections such as coughs, colds, flu, for example garlic, eucalyptus, marjoram, teatree.

Aperitifs: To stimulate the appetite: good examples include bergamot, ginger, orange.

Balance Thyroid Secretion: For balancing excessive secretions of thyroxine. Garlic is recommended. However the juice and bulb of both garlic and onion are more effective.

Carminative and Stomachics: For flatulence and nausea, for example cardamom, fennel, peppermint.

Cholagogues: For stimulating the gall bladder and thus the flow of bile, for example lavender, peppermint.

Cicatrisant: For stimulating the growth of healthy skin cells, helpful for burns, wounds and scars, for example chamomile, lavender, neroli.

Contain oestrogen-like substances: Some plants contain phyto-oestrogens which have been shown to help menopausal symptoms, for example fennel, hops, sage.

Contain Phyto-Steroids: These substances are said to resemble the male and female sex hormones and are found in frankincense and myrrh. Whether these essences exert a hormonal influence in humans is yet to be established.

Cytophylactics: For increasing the activity of white blood cells which help in our defence against infection, for example frankincense, lavender, rosemary.

Deodorant: Helpful for excessive perspiration and the cleansing of wounds, for example bergamot, cypress, lemongrass, sandalwood.

Depuratives or detoxifying agents: For helping to combat impurities in the blood and organs or to detoxify the system of metabolic wastes, for example angelica, juniper, fennel, lemon, rose otto.

Emmenagogues: For inducing menstruation and/or normalizing menstrual flow, for example chamomile, clary sage, lavender, rose otto.

Fungicidal: Helpful for fungal conditions of skin such as athlete's foot and ringworm, for example cedarwood, lavender, lemongrass, patchouli, teatree.

Galactogogues: For stimulating the flow of mothers milk, for example fennel, lemon grass.

Anti- Galactogogues: For reducing milk flow, for example peppermint, sage.

Hepatics: For strengthening, toning and stimulating the secretive functions of the liver, for example lemon, rosemary, peppermint.

Hormone Influencing: For a broad spectrum of problems associated with the female reproductive system, for example cypress, frankincense, geranium, hops, rose otto.

Hypnotics: For inducing sleep, for example chamomile, hops, neroli.

Hypertensive's (stimulate the circulation): Helpful for poor circulation and low blood pressure, for example black pepper, rosemary, thyme.

Hypotensive (lowers blood pressure): for example lavender, marjoram, ylang ylang.

Insect Repellant: To repel insects such as midgets and mosquitoes, for example lavender, eucalyptus, geranium, citronella, lemongrass.

Nervines (strengthens the nervous system): To reduce anxiety and stress which contribute to the development of cardiovascular disease, for example chamomile, lavender, neroli, clary sage, juniper, lemongrass, patchouli.

Normalising: For stimulating or relaxing, depending on the state of the individual, for example bergamot, geranium.

Parasiticides: (prevents and destroys parasites): For treating conditions such as head lice and scabies, for example eucalyptus, lavender, rosemary, tea tree.

Rubefacients: By stimulating the periphery circulation, such essences increase the blood supply to the affected area which in turn relieves congestion and inflammation for example black peeper, geranium and, rosemary.

Sedatives: For calming a jangled nervous system, for example clary sage, lavender, marjoram, sandalwood, vetiver.

Stimulants: To help restore energy levels depleted through illness or nervous fatigue, for example black pepper, coriander, peppermint, rosemary.

Tonics and Astringents (strengthens and tones the whole system): For varicose veins and hemorrhoids, for example cypress, geranium, lemon.

Uterine Tonics: For toning and regulating the female reproductive system and for excessive menstruation, for example frankincense, true mellisa, rose otto.

Vermifuges: For expelling intestinal worms, for example bergamot, lavender, lemon, peppermint, thyme.

Vulneraries: For helping to heal wounds, for example frankincense, lavender, marjoram, rosemary.

CHAPTER FOURTEEN

AROMA FAMILIES

Citrus: bergamot, grapefruit, lemon, lime, mandarin, orange.
Floral: geranium, chamomile, rose, lavender, neroli, ylang ylang.
Herbaceous: chamomile, lavender, peppermint, rosemary, marjoram, clary sage.
Camphoraceous: eucalyptus, cajuput, rosemary, peppermint, tea tree.
Spicy: coriander, black pepper, ginger, cardamom.
Resinous: frankincense, elemi, myrrh, galbanum.
Woody: cedarwood, sandalwood, pine, juniper, cypress.
Earthy: patchouli, vetiver.
Minty: peppermint, spearmint, and wintergreen.
Warmth: vanilla, benzoin, and tonka bean.
Exotic Florals: jasmine, ylang-ylang, or orchid.
Amber: amber
Animalistic: civet or musk.
A few natural essential oils belong to more than one group – a reflection of their complex chemical make-up.

CHAPTER FIFTEEN

ODOUR INTENITY OF ESSENTIAL OILS

Extremely High: carnation absolute, galbanum, mimosa absolute, oak moss, absolute, tagetes, valerian.

High: angelica, basil, black pepper, cardamom, chamomile, cinnamon, clove, elemi, eucalyptus, fennel, frankincense, ginger, hops, jasmine absolute, lemongrass, lime, Melissa, myrrh, nutmeg, patchouli, peppermint, rose, tea tree, thyme, vetiver, ylang ylang.

Fairly High: cajeput, clary sage, coriander, geranium, marjoram, myrtle, neroli, palmarosa, rosemary.

Medium: grapefruit, juniper, lavender, lemon, orange, petitgrain, pine, rose.

Low: bergamot, cedarwood, mandarin, sandalwood.

REMEDY REFERENCE

MIND:

ANGER - Bergamot, Orange, Petitgrain, Vertivert Ylang,

ANXIETY - Bergamot, Cedar Wood, Frankincense, Geranium, Lavender, Vetivert

CONFIDENCE - Bergamot, Orange, Rosemary

DEPRESSION - Bergamot Frankincense, Geranium, Lavender, Lemon, Orange, Ylang Ylang

FATIGUE - Basil, Bergamot, Black Pepper, Frankincense, Ginger, Lemon Peppermint, Rosemary, Vetivert

FEAR - Bergamot, Cedar Wood, Frankincense, Lemon, Orange, Vetivert

GRIEF - Frankincense, Vetivert

HAPPINESS and PEACE - Bergamot, Frankincense, Geranium, Lemon, Orange Ylang Ylang

INSECURITY - Bergamot, Cedar Wood, Frankincense, Vertivert

IRRITABILITY - Lavender

MEMORY and CONCENTRATION - Basil, Black Pepper, Lemon, Peppermint, Rosemary

PANIC and PANIC ATTACK - Frankincense, Lavender

STRESS - Bergamot, Frankincense, Geranium, Lavender, Vertivert, Ylang Ylang

BODY:

LYMPHATIC SYSTEM: - Diuretic essential oils help to accelerate lymph and tissue fluids circulation: - Lemon, Juniper Berry, and Geranium.

STIMULATING CIRULATORY SYSYTEM: - Black pepper, Rosemary and Ginger.

INCREASE PRODUCTION OF WHITE BLOOD CELLS: - Bergamot. Lavender, Lemon, and Rosemary,

ANTISEPTIC AND BACTERICIDAL OILS: - Lavender, Lemon and Tea Tree.

ENDOCRINE SYSTEM: - clary sage, lavender, geranium, peppermint, rosemary and frankincense.

NERVOUS SYSTEM: - bergamot, lavender and ylang ylang

MUSCULAR-SKELETAL SYSTEM: - lavender and rosemary

RUFEBACIENT: - rosemary and black pepper.

Geranium helps to stimulate the adrenal cortex, which indirectly influences the secretion of corticoid hormones.

Lavender and Ylang Ylang all help to lower blood pressure.

Bergamot, Lavender and Ylang Ylang are all Sedative and calming for the nervous system.

Peppermint, Lemon, and Rosemary all stimulate the nervous system.

CHAPTER SEVENTEEN

TEN ESSENTIAL OILS RECOMMENDED FOR YOUR HOME MEDICINE CABINET

BASIL – mental fatigue, nerve tonic, bronchitis, migraine, gout, loss of concentration, colds, asthma, fainting, to regulate menstrual cycle, coughs, digestive disorders, vomiting, wasp and insect bites.

BERGAMOT – acne, skin problems, herpes, tension, depression, stress, fevers, cystitis, restore appetite.

EUCALYPTUS - coughs, bronchitis, sore throat, sinusitis, rheumatism, skin infections, viral infections, migraine, herpes, mosquito repellant, strained muscles, urinary tract problems, cystitis.

JUNIPER – liver problems, purification, detoxifying, acne, urinary infections, diuretic, obesity, appetite, stimulant, period pains, eczema, psoriasis, ulcers, wounds, hangovers, rheumatism, cellulite, painful menstruations, sluggishness.

LAVENDER - burns, skin infections, skincare, cuts, wounds, acne, eczema, dermatitis, flu, nausea, stress, headaches, asthma, rheumatism, arthritis, cystitis, high blood pressure, muscle spasm, arthritis, muscular aches and pains, sunburn, fainting, insomnia, respiratory problems, allergies.

LEMON – digestive problems, sore throat, a nervous tonic, skin problems, insect repellent, arthritis, lowers blood pressure, colds, flu, sinusitis, gingivitis, nosebleeds, corns, warts and verrucas.

PEPPERMINT – nausea, flatulence, colic, indigestion, travel sickness, headaches, colds, flu, migraine, fevers, inflammation, arthritis, sinusitis, painful periods, mosquito repellant, asthma, bronchitis, fatigue, shock.

ROSEMARY - headaches, muscular strains, sports injuries, sprains, fatigue, dandruff, alopecia, stimulant, liver decongestant, rheumatism, colds, improves circulation, intestinal upsets, fluid retention, coughs, chest congestion.

TEA TREE – fungal infections, viral and bacterial infections, colds, flu, cold sores, acne, cystitis, candida, burns, athlete's foot, insect repellent, cuts, cold sores, stings, sore throats, sinusitis, chest problems, dandruff, verrucas and warts, to strengthen the immune system.

YLANG YLANG – anxiety, lowers blood pressure, depression, aphrodisiac, regulates and calms the heart, skincare, frigidity.

By investing in these TEN oils your family gains good health and happiness.

CHAPTER EIGHTEEN

ACTION OF ESSENTIAL OILS ON SKIN

Antiseptic: All essential oils are antiseptic to a greater or lesser degree, though good examples include eucalyptus, lavender, tea tree.

Anti-Inflammatory: Helpful for skin rashes and wounds, for example, chamomile, lavender, geranium.

Cicatrisant: Stimulates the growth of healthy skin cells and helpful for burns, wounds, and scars, for example, chamomile, lavender, neroli.

Deodorant: Helpful for excessive perspiration and the cleansing of wounds, for example, bergamot, cypress, lemongrass, sandalwood.

Fungicidal: Helpful for fungal conditions of the skin such as athlete's foot and ringworm, for example, cedarwood, lemongrass, patchouli.

Popular essential oils for skincare:

Lavender: Soothing and calming for irritated skin.

Tea Tree: Antibacterial properties for acne-prone skin.

Peppermint: Cooling and invigorating for scalp.

Chamomile: Soothing and calming for sensitive skin.

Lemon: Refreshing and cleansing properties.

Geranium: Balancing for oily skin.

Frankincense: Anti-aging properties.

Jojoba Oil: Moisturizing for all skin types.

Rosehip Oil: Rich in vitamin A, which can aid skin cell turnover and promote a brighter complexion.

Sun Protection: Daily use of sunscreen with SPF30(sun protection factor) or higher is crucial to prevent sun damage and hyperpigmentation, which can cause uneven skin tone.

Healthy Lifestyle: Maintaining a healthy diet rich in antioxidants and staying hydrated can contribute to overall skin health and radiance.

Consult a Dermatologist: A dermatologist can recommend evidence-based solutions for lightening dark spots or hyperpigmentation. They can also advise on safe and effective ingredients for your specific skin type.

Dilution: Essential oils are concentrated and must be diluted in a carrier oil like jojoba oil or coconut oil before applying to the skin.

list of essential oils to be avoided if you suffer from allergies or have a sensitive skin

Aniseed - Basil - Bay - Benzoin - Black Pepper - Cedarwood - Chamomile - Cinnamon - Citronella - - Clary Sage - Clove - Fennel - Ginger - Juniper - Lemon - Lemongrass - Lime - Nutmeg - Orange - - Peppermint - Pine - Spearmint - Tea Tree - Thyme - Ylang Ylang

Note: It is better to get professional advice to use essential oils during pregnancy

CHAPTER NINETEEN

SMELL ACTS ON THE BRAIN DIRECTLY

Essential Oils, or essences as they are also called, are highly concentrated substances extracted from various parts of aromatic plants and trees. The chemistry of the essential oils is complex. Most consist of hundreds of components, such as terpenes, alcohols, aldehydes and esters. For this reason single oil can help a wide variety of disorders.

Due to its tiny molecular structure, natural essential oils applied to the skin can be absorbed into the blood stream.

When inhaled, they pass through the tiny air sacs in the lungs to the surrounding blood capillaries by the process of diffusion. Once in the blood stream the aromatic molecules interact with the body's chemistry to activate the body's own innate self-healing ability.

Essential oils initiate chemical changes in the body when the essential oil enters the bloodstream and reacts with hormones and enzymes.

Essential oils have a physiological effect on systems of the body.

Essential oils have a psychological effect when the odor of the oil is inhaled.

Essential oils are absorbed into the blood stream; through the skin and via the respiratory system.

CHAPTER TWENTY

ANISEED

Aniseed oil is good for the digestive system, it is also a general tonic to the circulatory system and the respiratory tract. It helps to calm the nerves of tense and anxiety ridden people. It also calms menstrual pains and eases nauseous migraines, while stimulating the lungs to expel phlegm.

Burners and vaporizers

In vapor therapy, aniseed oil is useful for asthma, colds and all breathing problems, as well as quelling nausea and vomiting.

Drops of oil on a handkerchief

When used on a handkerchief to smell at, it is useful for settling digestive problems and can also benefit migraine and vertigo sufferers.

Aniseed blends well with: cardamom, coriander, dill, fennel, mandarin, petitgrain and rosewood.

CHAPTER TWENTY-ONE

BASIL

Basil oil is very beneficial oil and can be helpful not only for headaches and migraines, but also has an uplifting effect on depression.

It is effective in digestive disorders, ranging from nausea to hiccups, and for infections in the respiratory tract.

It is useful for wasp and insect bites, particularly that of mosquitoes.

Burners and vaporizers

In vapor therapy, basil oil can be used for migraines, headaches and to help increase concentration and clear the mind.

Blended in the bath

When adding basil oil to a warm bath, it can help relieve gout and arthritis, as well as muscular and menstrual pains.

Basil oil blends well with: bergamot, black pepper, cedarwood, fennel, ginger, geranium, grapefruit, lavender, lemon, marjoram, neroli and verbena.

CHAPTER TWENTY-TWO

BAY

Bay oil is calming and warming, effective on emotions and general aches and pains, including rheumatic pains. It also settles the digestive system, excess gas and also acts as a tonic on the liver and kidneys.

In small amounts it has a stimulating effect, while larger doses produce a sedating effect. Bay essential oil is also helpful with hair and scalp conditions and is mostly used to combat hair loss and is used with success in treating sprains, strains and bruises.

Burners and vaporizers

In vapor therapy, bay oil can be used for an infection, for fever and general aches and pains. It can also trigger inspiration and has a calming effect on the mind.

Blended massage oil and in the bath

As a blended massage oil or diluted in the bath, bay oil can assist with calming emotions and relieving aches and pains, especially when combined with rose and juniper, but care must be taken as it can irritate the mucus membranes.

Bay oil blends well with: cedarwood, coriander, eucalyptus, geranium, ginger, juniper, lavender, lemon, orange, rose, rosemary, thyme and ylang-ylang.

CHAPTER TWENTY-THREE

BENZOIN

Benzoin oil's greatest benefit lies in that it has a calming effect on the nervous and digestive systems, a warming effect on circulation problems and a toning effect on the respiratory tract. It furthermore boosts the pancreas, which in turns helps digestion, and is thought to be involved in controlling blood sugar, which makes it valuable for sufferers of diabetes. The effect it has on the skin is to improve elasticity, helping cracked skin, while aiding the healing of sores and wounds and at the same time reducing redness, irritation and itching.

Burners and vaporizers

In vapor therapy Benzoin oil can be used for the nervous system, calming and bringing comfort to the depressed and emotionally exhausted.

Blended massage oil or in the bath

Benzoin oil can be used in blended massage oil, or diluted in the bath to assist with general aches and pains, arthritis and rheumatism, as well as chronic bronchitis and coughing. Poor circulation will also benefit from this oil, as well as stiff muscles. It also has a calming effect and helps to ease depression. It furthermore gives the skin a general boost by increasing elasticity, reducing redness, irritation and itchiness, while helping wound healing.

Blended in a cream

Benzoin oil is a good remedy for dry, cracked skin, cuts and wounds, as well as for acne and irritable and itching skin, while at the same time improving elasticity.

Benzoin oil blends well with: bergamot, coriander, frankincense, juniper, lavender, lemon, myrrh, orange, petitgrain, rose and sandalwood.

CHAPTER TWENTY-FOUR

BERGAMOT

Bergamot ia a good oil to help with depression, SAD (Seasonal Affected Disorder) or generally feeling just a bit off, lacking in self-confidence or feeling shy then consider bergamot oil.

It also has antiseptic qualities that are useful for skin complaints, such as acne, oily skin conditions, eczema and psoriasis and can also be used on cold sores, chicken pox and wounds.

It is effective in stimulating the liver, stomach and spleen and has a superb antiseptic effect on urinary tract infections and inflammations such as cystitis.

Burners and vaporizers

In vapor therapy, bergamot oil can be used for depression, feeling fed-up, respiratory problems, colds and flu, PMS and SAD.

Blended massage oil or in the bath

It can be used in blended massage oil, or diluted in a bath to assist with stress, tension, SAD, PMS, skin problems, compulsive eating, postnatal depression, colds and flu, anxiety, depression, feeling fed-up and anorexia nervosa.

Blended in base cream

As a constituent in a blended base cream bergamot oil can be used for wounds and cuts, psoriasis, oily skin, scabies, eczema, acne, cold sores as well as chicken pox.

Bergamot blends well with: clary sage, cypress, frankincense, geranium, jasmine, mandarin, nutmeg, orange, rosemary, sandalwood, vetiver and ylang-ylang.

BLACK PEPPER

This warming oil can be used to a great effect to help blood circulation and specifically to help with muscle tone, aching limbs and rheumatoid arthritis. It further helps to promote digestion, the colon as well as the kidneys.

Burners and vaporizers

In vapor therapy, black pepper oil can be used to help add warmth to chills and colds and to create an atmosphere of 'getting things done'.

Blended oil or in the bath

Black pepper oil can be used in blended massage oil, or diluted in a bath, to assist with circulation, bruises, rheumatoid arthritis and muscular aches and pains.

Blended in base cream

As a constituent in a blended cream is can be used for tired aching limbs, sore muscles, rheumatoid arthritis, stimulating the appetite and to help sort out bowel problems. In small quantities it can be used to reduce high temperatures. It increases circulation to the skin and is therefore helpful in restoring proper functioning of the skin.

Black pepper blends well with: bergamot, clarysage, clove, coriander, fennel, frankincense, geranium, ginger, grapefruit, lavender, juniper, lemon, lime, mandarin, sage, sandalwood and ylang-ylang.

CHAPTER TWENTY-SIX

CAJUPUT

The greatest benefit of cajuput oil lies in its antiseptic properties for the respiratory tract and the urinary system, the combating of infections such as colds, bronchitis and laryngitis and its pain relieving properties for headaches, earache, toothache, gout and rheumatism.

Burners and vaporizers

Cajuput oil can be used in vapor therapy for the respiratory tract, relieving infections and pain. It also helps to promote clear thoughts and dispels a feeling of sluggishness.

Massage oil

It helps for pain relief and is useful in gout, rheumatism, arthritis and general aches and pains. Its antispasmodic properties make it useful for treating painful periods, delayed menses and spasmodic dysmenorrhoea.

In the bath

In the bath cajuput oil can help to reduce fevers by exerting a cooling influence - but take care not to irritate the mucus membranes.

Blended cream

When used as part of a formulation, it can be helpful to sort out persistent and chronic conditions such as acne and psoriasis.

Cajuput oil blends well with: angelica, bergamot, cloves, geranium, lavender, and thyme.

CAMPHOR

Camphor is a balancing oil; it can sedate the nerves and uplift apathy. It can help with feeling cold and reduces inflammation. It is used with great effect to repel insects such as flies and moths.

It also has a positive effect in colds and flu, infectious diseases, bronchitis, coughs, and can assist with muscular pains, rheumatism, sprains, arthritis etc.

Burners and vaporizers

In vapor therapy camphor oil can be used with great effect for the heart, clearing the lungs and boosting circulation, as well as calming nervous diseases and for convalescence.

Cold compresses

For bruises and sprains, cold compresses are effective.

In a cream

Although very small amounts of camphor oil would be included in any formulation, it does have value in fighting inflammatory conditions and reducing redness, making it useful for treating acne, burns and sore chapped hands.

Camphor oil blends well with: basil, cajuput, chamomile, lavender and melissa

CHAPTER TWENTY-EIGHT

CARROTSEED

Carrot seed oil's purifying on the liver and the digestive system. It is also a great help in the treatment of muscular aches and pains, skin problems and respiratory ailments.

Burners and vaporizers

Carrot seed oil can be used in vapor therapy for relieving stress, boosting the liver, the digestive and respiratory systems, as well as for muscle pains. It does not have an over-powering smell, but this earthy smell will help to "ground" a person while fighting stress and exhaustion.

Creams and lotions

It has nearly magical rejuvenating effect on the skin, to not only soften and smooth the skin, but to assist with cell growth and skin rejuvenation.

Blended massage oil or in the bath

As a blended massage oil or diluted in the bath, carrot seed oil can assist with muscle pains and in boosting the respiratory tract, while detoxifying the body and boosting the manufacture of red blood cells.

Carrot seed oil blends well with: bergamot, juniper, lavender, lemon, lime, cedarwood, geranium, as well as all citrus and spicy oils.

CHAPTER TWENTY-NINE

CEDARWOOD

Cedarwood oil calma and soothes nerves. It relieves skin and hair problems and is important in easing conditions of a respiratory nature. It also clears urinary infections, rheumatism and arthritis.

Burners and vaporizers

In vapor therapy, cedarwood oil can be used for arthritis, bronchitis, rheumatism, respiratory problems, as a general tonic and as an insect repellant.

Blended massage oil or in the bath

Cedarwood can be used in blended massage oil, or diluted in the bath to assist with asthma, bronchitis, respiratory problems, catarrh, cystitis, painful joints, oily skin and dandruff. Care must be taken that it does not cause irritation to the mucus membranes.

In a cream

When diluted in a cream, cedarwood oil is of great value to combat oily skin and related problems, as well as dermatitis and psoriasis, while bringing relief to the scalp from dandruff.

Cedarwood oil blends well with: benzoin, bergamot, cinnamon, cypress, frankincense, jasmine, juniper, lavender, lemon.

CINNAMON

Cinnamon oil's benefit lies in its toning and calming effect on the respiratory tract, the nervous system, and in the easing of colds and influenza, as well as period pains.

It also calms the digestive system and helps with rheumatism and arthritis. Although traditionally used for clearing warts, it is not recommended to be used in skin care products.

Burners and vaporizers

In vapor therapy, cinnamon oil can be used in acute bronchitis and colds, as well as sneezing and to help lift depression and a feeling of weakness.

Blended oil or in the bath

Cinnamon oil can be used in blended massage oil or diluted in the bath, to assist with bronchitis, diarrhea, chills, infections, flu, rheumatism and arthritis. Due to its very powerful antiseptic properties it is good for fighting any infectious diseases. It furthermore has great value in calming spasms of the digestive tract, nausea and vomiting. It stimulates secretion of digestive juices, while easing muscular and joint pains associated with rheumatism and arthritis. Care should however be taken not to irritate the skin and mucus membranes.

In a cream or lotion

As with the above, cinnamon oil can help with digestion, rheumatism and arthritic pain. It helps to fight colds and flu when used in the formulation of a cream or lotion.

Cinnamon oil blends well with: lavender, rosemary and thyme.

CHAPTER THIRTY-ONE

CITRONELLA

Citronella oil is an effective insecticide, but its antiseptic properties make it a great boon when wishing to clear a sickroom. It also has an excellent effect on clearing the mind. It may be used for combating excessive perspiration and for balancing oily skin, as well as fighting intestinal parasites and bringing down fever.

Burners and vaporizers

In a diffuser, citronella oil can be used as an insect repellent, for colds and flu, for clearing the mind and to refresh the sickroom. In Africa, where malaria is a great problem, citronella oil is used to a great extent to keep the disease carrying mosquitoes at bay.

In a cream or lotion

When included in a cream or lotion, citronella oil is most useful to keep the tropical wearer safe from mosquitoes that cause malaria. It also has a dramatic freshening effect on tired sweaty feet.

Citronella oil blends well with: bergamot, geranium, lemon, orange, lavender and pine.

CHAPTER THIRTY-TWO

CLOVE

Clove oil is useful for its disinfecting properties, relieving of pain, especially toothache, arthritis and rheumatism. It is effective when used for complaints of the digestion system. It is also of use for skin problems, especially for skin sores and leg ulcers and as an insect repellent.

Burners and vaporizersIn vapor therapy, clove oil can be useful for bronchitis and dizziness and to help lift depression, while strengthening memory and fighting weakness and lethargy.

Massage oil

Clove oil can be used in a blended massage oil to assist with diarrhea, bronchitis, chills, colds, muscular numbness, spasms, rheumatism and arthritis. For toothache the outer jaw can be massaged with this oil. Use a low dilution of less than 1%.

In cream or lotion

When used in a cream or lotion, the positive effects of clove oil are the same as those of massage oil and can furthermore help to sort out leg ulcers and skin sores. Use in low dilution of less than 1%.

Mouthwash

Clove oil can be included at a low rate as part of a mouthwash for toothache.

Clove oil blends well with: basil, benzoin, cinnamon, lavender, ginger, sandalwo

CHAPTER THIRTY-THREE

CYPRESS

Cypress oil has a calming and soothing effect on the nerves, ii is valuable as a vasoconstrictor, useful in the treatment of excessive discharge of fluids and beneficial for the respiratory tract.

Burners and vaporizers

It is useful in vapor therapy for all breathing difficulty, such as asthma, emphysema, whooping cough and bronchitis. It also helps to calm the mind and dispel anger.

Blended massage oil or in the bath

Cypress oil can be used as massage oil or diluted in the bath for arthritis, asthma, cellulite, cramps, diarrhea, sweaty feet, rheumatism, varicose veins, heavy menstruation and menopause.

Lotions and creams

In a cream base, cypress oil can be used for varicose and broken veins, as well as clearing an oily and congested skin.

Cold compress

Used diluted on a cold compress, it is very effective for a nosebleed.

Foot bath

If it is added to a footbath, it will help control perspiration with its astringent and deodorant properties.

Cypress oil blends well with: bergamot, clary sage, lavender, juniper, pine, marjoram, sandalwood, rosemary, frankincense and all the citrus oils.

CHAPTER THIRTY-FOUR

DILL

Gripe water is often made of the fresh herb and given to babies and children for colic or other digestive disorders, but the dill oil should not be used for this purpose, as it is too powerful.

Dill oil helps to overcome the feeling of being overwhelmed and is also helpful for digestive problems in adults, easing flatulence, constipation and hiccups.

It eases the mind, calms headaches and helps with excess sweating due to nervous tension. It can also stimulate milk flow in nursing mothers, while promoting the healing of wounds.

Summary

Dill oil calms and soothes the nerves and is helpful for digestive problems in adults, while helping the healing of wounds.

Burners and vaporizers

Dill essential oil can be used in vapor therapy for nervous tension, colic and indigestion and especially when you experience a feeling of being overwhelmed and in crisis.

Massage oil or in the bath

It can be a most helpful aid to calm and promote proper digestion, easing flatulence, as well as constipation and hiccups.

In a cream or lotion

When blended in a cream or lotion, it can have a very powerful effect on the healing of wounds.

Dill oil blends well with: bergamot, caraway, nutmeg and citrus oils.

CHAPTER THIRTY-FIVE

EUCALYPTUS

Eucalyptus oil is used for headaches, fevers, ailments of the respiratory tract, muscular aches and pains and in skin care. It has a soothing and calming effect on the whole body and helps with the immune system.

The oil is also effective against bacteria - especially staphylococci, and has a refreshing and stimulating action on the mind, helping to improve concentration.

Burners and vaporizers

In vapor therapy, eucalyptus oil may be used for: frequent sneezing, hay fever, flu, respiratory problems, as insect repellant, headaches and for helping to improve concentration.

Blended massage oil or in the bath

Eucalyptus oil can be used in blended massage oil or diluted in the bath, to assist with arthritis, asthma, bronchitis, mucous congestion, colds, headaches, rheumatism, sinusitis, catarrh, fatigue and muscular aches and pains.

In a cream or lotion

Apart from giving pain relief to muscular spasms and rheumatism, eucalyptus oil can also help speed up the healing of slow healing wounds and ulcers, calm skin eruptions and clear congested skin.

Eucalyptus oil can be used neat on the skin for insect bites or wounds, but care should be taken when doing so.

When much diluted eucalyptus oil is added to a gargle, it can be used for soothing a sore throat.

Eucalyptus oil blends well with: benzoin, thyme, lavender, lemongrass, lemon and pine.

CHAPTER THIRTY-SIX

FENNEL

Fennel oil is a remedy for digestive complaints such as flatulence, constipation, colic, nausea, vomiting, anorexia, dyspepsia and hiccups. It is also used in cases of obesity, as it promotes that 'full feeling' and has a diuretic effect that helps to disperse cellulite.

For the mind, it adds courage and strength in the face of adversity. It has a cleansing and toning effect on the skin, helping with bruises, sorting out overly oily skin and to fight wrinkles in more mature complexions (possibly due to the estrogenic properties of the oil).

It has a toning effect on the spleen and liver, that helps with the results of excess drink and food. It is also used for increasing insufficient milk in nursing mothers - but for boosting breast milk, rather use the fresh herb, since the oil contains very high concentrations of trans-anethole.

Summary

Fennel oil's greatest benefits lie in its easing of the digestive system, helping with obesity and toning the skin.

Burners and vaporizers

In vapor therapy, fennel oil is used as an appetite stimulant in cases of anorexia, and to boost courage and strength in the face of adversity.

Blended massage oil or in the bath

Fennel oil can be used as blended massage oil or diluted in the bath for helping to fix a bloated stomach, excess wind, colic, constipation and other digestive problems. It also acts as a diuretic, to remove excess water and to start breaking down cellulite.

Creams and lotions

Used in a base cream or lotion, fennel oil can be helpful for general skin care and especially for dispersing bruises, livening a dull complexion, clearing an oily skin and fighting wrinkles in mature skins. It is also useful for removing cellulite, to fight rheumatism and helps with edema.

Fennel oil blends well with: geranium, lavender, rose and sandalwood.

FRANKINCENSE

Frankincense calms and soothes the whole body and mind. It eases all aches and pains, clears the lungs and acts as a skin tonic.

Burners and vaporizers

In vapor therapy, frankincense can be used for bronchitis, colds, coughs and voice loss, as well as to calm the mind, reduce anxiety and cultivating internal peace and placing past obsessive states into perspective.

Blended massage oil or in the bath

Frankincense oil can be used in blended massage oil or diluted in the bath for colds, coughs, bronchitis, rheumatism, chilliness, poor circulation, exhaustion, nightmares, heavy periods, respiratory problems and mucus congestion. It also has a good astringent effect on the skin and perks up older more mature skin and helps wounds, sores and ulcers heal properly.

Creams and lotions

Frankincense oil can be added to a base cream or lotion to help with general skin tone and condition while reducing oily skin, rejuvenating more mature skin, while at the same time helping wounds, ulcers and sores heal better.

Wash or use as a compress

To promote healing and prevent ugly scarring on wounds, add a few drops to the water when washing the wound. For cracked skin and bed sores, apply gently (suitably diluted) directly on to affected areas or use as a compress.

Frankincense oil blends well with: benzoin, sandalwood, lavender, myrrh, pine, orange, bergamot and lemon

CHAPTER THIRTY-EIGHT

GERANIUM

Geranium oil has a all-over balancing effect on the mind and this uplifting property also extends to the effect it has on the skin - where it helps to create balance between oily and dry skin. It helps to sort out emotions - where it helps to relieve feelings of stress and anxiety, and also works on the adrenal cortex, which has a balancing effect on the hormone system.

The strong smell is particularly good to ward off mosquitoes and head lice.

Burners and vaporizers

In vapor therapy geranium oil can be used to help relieve stress, mild depression, PMS, anxiety and tension, menopausal problems and for general energizing.

Blended massage oil or in the bath

Geranium oil can be used in blended massage oil, or diluted in a bath to assist with PMS, depression, stress, anxiety and tension, fluid retention, edema, eczema, shingles, cellulite, bruises, insect repellent, ringworm, hemorrhoids and menstrual irregularities.

Blended in cream or lotion

As a constituent in a blended base cream, geranium oil can be used for eczema, repelling insects, shingles, burns and scalds, cellulite, ringworm, bruises and engorgement of the breasts.

It will help to balance the oil production of the skin and help keep it supple, while the cicatrisant properties ensure that it is helpful in wound healing, including burns, wounds and ulcers.

Geranium oil can also be diluted in shampoo to help with head lice.

Geranium oil blends well with: angelica, basil, bergamot, carrotseed, cedarwood, citronella, clarysage, grapefruit, jasmine, lavender, lime, neroli, orange and rosemary.

CHAPTER THIRTY-NINE

GINGER

Ginger oil is well suited to help ease colds and flu, nausea, motion sickness, morning sickness, muscle aches and pains, as well as poor circulation and arthritic pain. Its warming qualities are good to use for feelings of loneliness and winter depression, and its energizing properties make it a good aphrodisiac.

Burners and vaporizers

In vapor therapy, it can be used to help relieve catarrh, lethargy, nausea, colds, flu and feeling of loneliness.

Blended oil or in the bath

In blended massage oil or diluted in the bath, it can be used for arthritis, rheumatism, lethargy, nausea, colds and flu, muscle aches, poor circulation and digestive upsets.

Blended in base cream

As a part of a cream or lotion it can be used for arthritis, muscle aches, rheumatism and also to help with poor circulation and to disperse bruises.

When used with hot compresses, ginger oil can be used for arthritis, rheumatism, muscle aches and digestive upsets.

For ease of use, applying a drop of oil to a handkerchief for quick inhalation, it can be used for nausea, morning sickness, indigestion, colds, flu and travel sickness.

Ginger oil blends well with: bergamot, frankincense, neroli, rose, sandalwood and ylang-ylang.

CHAPTER FORTY

JUNIPER

Juniper oil is very valuable oil and can be used in cases of nervous tension and anxiety, for the urinary tract, for over-eating and obesity, for eliminating uric acid and for skin care. The affinity to the urino-genital tract was further shown when studies revealed that it enhances glomerular filtration, thereby causing the excretion of more amounts of potassium, sodium and chlorine - especially helpful when the prostate gland is enlarged.

Burners and vaporizers

In vapor therapy juniper oil can be used for the treatment of addictions, nervous tension, hangovers, over-indulgence of food and to stimulate the nervous system and bolster the spirit in challenging situations.

Blended massage oil or in the bath

Juniper oil can be used as blended massage oil or diluted in the bath, for colic in adults, arthritis, cellulite, nervous tension, cystitis, pain in passing urine, gout, hangover, swollen joints, liver problems, muscle fatigue and overweight.

Lotions and creams

When used in a base cream or lotion, juniper oil can be useful for an oily skin and acne, as well as weeping eczema, dermatitis, blocked pores, psoriasis and other inflammatory skin ailments.

Juniper oil can be used diluted on a compress for arthritis, eczema and general infections.

Juniper oil blends well with: cedarwood, cypress, geranium, grapefruit, lavender, bergamot, lime, vetiver, clarysage and lemongrass.

CHAPTER FORTY-ONE

LAVENDER

Lavender oil is one of the most versatile oils and is handy to have around the house, as it can be used for such a variety of problems. It not only helps with nervous conditions, it is useful for the digestive system, the respiratory tract and skin problems, it also helps with muscle aches and pains and arthritis and rheumatism.

Burners and vaporizers

In vapor therapy, lavender oil can be useful for allergies, anorexia, dizziness, sleeplessness (also in children), hay fever, headaches, depression, trauma, anxiety, hysteria, fear, nightmares, irritability, nervous tension and as an insect repellant. Apart from that it can assist to lift depression, help in crisis situations, sooth irritability and relieve stress and thereby help with tense muscles and muscle spasms.

Blended massage oil or in the bath

Lavender oil can be used as a massage oil or diluted in the bath, for abdominal pains, allergies, anorexia, arthritis, bowel disorders, fatigue, hay fever, headaches, insomnia, moodiness, trauma, anxiety, depression, hysteria, nightmares, fear, irritability, nervous tension, stress and just for the plain pleasure of relaxing in such a fragrant surrounding.

Lavender oil can be used as a wash or on a cotton bud for acne, insect bites, carbuncles, bruises, chilblains, dandruff and lice.

On a cold compress, lavender oil can be used for: arthritis, eczema and sores.

Cream or lotion

When it is used in a cream or lotion, it is most helpful with relieving burns, its cicatrisant properties help the skin heal faster and the cytophylactic properties will help it do so with less scarring. The soothing and anti-inflammatory action of lavender oil will also have a balancing action on the skin and can be used for dermatitis, eczema, psoriasis, boils, carbuncles and acne. When employing the anti-inflammatory action of this oil, use in concentrations of less than 1%. Furthermore it will help ease the pain of sunburn and sunstroke and will also counter the itching effect of insect bites.

Lavender oil blends well with: cedarwood, clary sage, geranium, pine, nutmeg and all the citrus oils.

CHAPTER FORTY-TWO

LEMON

Lemon oil helps to fight against infections, aids the digestive system, soothes headaches, migraines and muscular problems and clears greasy skin and hair.

Burners and vaporizers

In vapor therapy, lemon oil can be used for colds, voice loss, flu, depression, stress, lack of energy and fatigue. It furthermore relieves irritation and also helps improve concentration, lifts the spirits, clears the mind and helps in decision making.

Blended massage oil or in the bath

Lemon oil can be used in blended massage oils or diluted in the bath to assist with digestive problems, lack of energy, fatigue, infections, flu, obesity, overweight, rheumatism, depression, stress and as a general tonic.

Lotions and creams

Lemon oil can be used in a cream or lotion to clear congested skin. The astringent properties are great for oily skin conditions. The antiseptic effect of lemon oil on the other hand, helps to treat any cuts, boils and minor wounds. The rubefacient action of the oil further helps to sort out cellulite, as well as helping with acne.

If dispersed in a very diluted form in warm water, it can be used as a mouth wash or gargle to sort out mouth ulcers.

Lemon oil blends well with: lavender, rose, sandalwood, benzoin, eucalyptus, geranium, fennel, juniper.

CHAPTER FORTY-THREE

LEMONGRASS

Lemongrass oil has great benefits as a muscle and skin toner, and revitalizes the body and mind, helps with infections and keeps the family pet flea and tick free and smelling nice.

Burners and vaporizers

In vapor therapy, Lemongrass oil can be used for nervousness and as an insect repellant. It is also great to revive the mind when feeling lethargic and to energize as well as relieving fatigue.

Blended massage oil or in the bath

Lemongrass oil can be used in blended massage oil or diluted in the bath to assist with cellulite, digestive problems, as a diuretic, for infections, nervousness, for over exerted ligaments and as a general tonic.

Cream or lotion

When used in a lotion or a cream, it has value in clearing cellulite, as well as toning the skin, opening blocked pores and helping with acne. The antiseptic properties are useful in treating athlete's foot and other fungal infections.

Note: Although some people may have an allergic reaction to lemongrass oil, most people do not show an allergy when it is used in concentrations lower than 3%.

Lemongrass oil blends well with: basil, cedarwood, coriander, geranium, jasmine, lavender and tea tree.

CHAPTER FORTY-FOUR

LIME

Lime oil is useful to cool fevers associated with colds, sore throats and flu and aids the immune system while easing coughs, bronchitis and sinusitis, as well as helping asthma. Lime oil can stimulate and refresh a tired mind and helps with depression.

It can be helpful for arthritis, rheumatism and poor circulation, as well as for obesity and cellulite and has an astringent and toning action to clear oily skin and acne, and also helps with herpes, insect bites and cuts.

Summary

Lime oil is beneficial to the immune system, easing infection in the respiratory tract and relieving pain in muscles and joints, while revitalizing a tired mind and banishing the feeling of apathy, anxiety and depression.

Burners and vaporizers

In vapor therapy, lime oil can be used to lift depression and energize a tired mind, while easing breathing and assisting the digestion.

Blended massage oil or in the bath

Lime oil can be used as a massage oil or diluted in the bath, to help with painful muscles and joints, respiratory problems and cellulite, as well as when colds and flu strike.

Cream or lotion

When used in a cream or lotion, it is helpful to clear oily congested skin and is also often used to help fight cellulite and remove the cottage cheese effect from the skin.

Lime essential oil blends well with: neroli, lavender, clary sage and ylang-ylang.

CHAPTER FORTY-FIVE

MANDARIN

Mandarin oil is soothing to the nervous system and has a tonic effect on the digestive system, while helping flatulence, diarrhea and constipation. It is also useful for the skin and is used to help with stretch marks, increasing circulation and reducing fluid retention.

It can boost the digestive system, reduce retention, increase circulation and sooth the nervous system and relieve stress and tension.

Burners and vaporizers

In vapor therapy, mandarin oil can help with soothing the nervous system and thereby reduce stress and tension, while also boosting the digestive system.

Blended massage oil or in the bath

As a blended massage oil or diluted in the bath, mandarin oil can assist the nervous system, reduce flatulence, diarrhea, constipation, and other digestive complaints, but also increase circulation to the skin, reduce fluid retention and help prevent stretch marks.

Cream or lotion

In a lotion or cream, it is used to help prevent stretch marks when pregnant, while increasing circulation and reducing fluid retention.

Mandarin oil blends well with: basil, black pepper, chamomile, cinnamon, clove, frankincense, grapefruit, jasmine, lemon, neroli, patchouli and sandalwood

MARJORAM

Marjoram oil has a warming action and calms emotions, relieves anxiety as well as stress and helps to calms hyperactive people. It has good muscle relaxant properties and the pain killing properties are useful for rheumatic pains as well as sprains, strains and spasms, as well as swollen joints and painful muscles.

It soothes the digestive system and helps with cramps, indigestion, constipation and flatulence and has a beneficial action on colds, sinusitis, bronchitis and asthma.

As a general relaxant, marjoram oil is used for headaches, migraines and insomnia and although it can diminish sexual desire, it is great for treating delayed, painful or scanty monthly periods as well as menstrual cramps.

Summary

Marjoram oil can be beneficial in cases of nervous tension, respiratory congestion, painful muscles and joints, digestive problems and menstrual disorders.

Burners and vaporizers

In vapor therapy, marjoram oil can be used for asthma, bronchitis, poor circulation, coughs, physical exhaustion, headaches, tension, insomnia, sinusitis, anxiety, nervous tension and stress.

Blended massage oil or in the bath

As a blended massage oil or diluted in the bath, marjoram oil can be used for asthma, arthritis, back pain, bronchitis, poor circulation, colds, coughs, detoxification, physical exhaustion, fatigue, headaches, tension, heartburn, insomnia, painful periods, migraine, muscular pains and spasms, rheumatism, sinusitis, anxiety, stress and grief.

Creams and lotions

Since it is a warming oil it is useful to counter chilblains and to disperse bruises.

Marjoram oil blends well with: lavender, cypress, cedarwood, chamomile, bergamot, eucalyptus and tea tree.

CHAPTER FORTY-SEVEN

MYRRH

Myrrh oil is effective against excessive mucus in the lungs and helps to clear ailments such as colds, catarrh, coughs, sore throats and bronchitis. It is used for diarrhea, dyspepsia, flatulence and haemorrhoids. It is very good for mouth and gum disorders, such as mouth ulcers, pyorrhea, gingivitis, spongy gums and sore throats. On the skin, it is used with great success on boils, skin ulcers, bedsores, chapped and cracked skin, ringworm, weeping wounds, eczema and athlete's foot. Furthermore, it is of great help to promote menstruation and for relieving painful periods and to ease difficult labor in childbirth.

Summary

Myrrh oil is of great benefit to the respiratory tract, the digestive system, for gum and mouth disorders, in skin care, as well as urino-genital and gynecological problems.

Burners and vaporizers

In vapor therapy, myrrh oil can be useful with bronchitis, catarrh, colds and coughs. It is also great for enhancing spirituality and is most useful when meditating.

Blended massage oil or in the bath

In a blended massage oil or diluted in the bath, myrrh oil is great for bronchitis, catarrh, colds, coughs and infections, as well as the variety of female problems listed above. It also has a wonderful effect on the skin.

Mouthwash

It can be included when mixing a mouthwash for all dental infections.

Cold compress

Myrrh oil can be used diluted on a cold compress for sores, skin care and wounds.

Cream or lotion

When used in a cream or lotion, amazing results are achieved in the treatment of chronic wounds and ulcers. It accelerates wound healing and sorts out athlete's foot, as well as weeping eczema. Bedsores, deeply chapped and cracked skin, boils, carbuncles, acne and all other skin ailments show dramatic results when myrrh oil is used to treat them, and it can also be applied with a cotton bud directly on sores, wounds and other skin infections.

Myrrh oil blends well with: benzoin, frankincense, lavender, sandalwood and clove.

CHAPTER FORTY-EIGHT

ORANGE

Orange oil can be used effectively on the immune system, as well as for colds and flu and to eliminate toxins from the body.

It is a good diuretic and is most useful in balancing water retention and obesity. Its lymphatic stimulant action further helps to balance water processes, detoxification, aiding the immune system and general well-being.

For the digestive system, orange oil can help with constipation, dyspepsia and as a general tonic. It is also useful in cases of nervous tension and stress.

Burners and vaporizers

In vapor therapy, orange oil can help with colds and flu, nervous tension and stress and helps to create a feeling of happiness and warmth, while helping children fall asleep at night.

Blended massage oil and in a bath

As a blended massage oil or added to a bath, it assists with colds and flu, eliminates toxins, boost the lymphatic and immune system and helps ease nervous tension and stress.

Cream or lotion

When used in a cream or lotion it also assists the lymphatic system, helping to detoxify a congested skin and although it is a good general skin tonic, it is great for older more mature skin, dealing with dermatitis, as well as acne and soothing a dry irritated skin. The general tonic action seems to stem from the action it has on supporting collagen formation in the skin, which is required for a healthy, young-looking skin.

Orange oil blends well with: blackpepper, cinnamon, cloves, ginger, frankincense, sandalwood and vetiver.

CHAPTER FORTY-NINE

PALMAROSA

Palmarosa oil calms the mind, yet has an uplifting effect, while clearing muddled thinking. It is used to counter physical and nervous exhaustion, stress-related problems and nervousness. It is most useful during convalescence and cools the body of fever, while aiding the digestive system, helping to clear intestinal infection, digestive atonia and anorexia nervosa. It is effective in relieving sore, stiff muscles. Palmarosa oil moisturizes the skin, while balancing the hydration levels and stimulating cell regeneration. It balances production of sebum, to keep the skin supple and elastic and is valuable for use with acne, dermatitis, preventing scarring, rejuvenating and regenerating the skin, as well as fighting minor skin infections, sore tired feet and athlete's foot.

Summary

Palmarosa oil could be used with good effect on the skin, for nervous and stress-related problems and for the digestive system.

Burners and vaporizers

In vapor therapy, palmarosa oil can help during convalescence. It relieves fatigue, nervousness, exhaustion and stress, while having an uplifting effect on the mind and clearing muddled thoughts.

Blended massage oil or in the bath

In a blended massage oil or diluted in the bath, palmarosa oil can be used on convalescent patients, to fight exhaustion, fatigue, nervousness, stress, bolstering the digestive system, while boosting the health of the skin.

Wash lotions and creams and used neat

Palmarosa oil can help clear up infections and prevent scarring when added to the water used to wash the wound. When included in creams and lotions, it has a moisturizing and hydrating effect on the skin, which is great to fight wrinkles. It also balances the natural secretion of sebum, which keeps the skin supple and elastic.

On cellular level, it helps with the formation of new tissue and for that reason is great for rejuvenating and regenerating the skin. It is most useful when fighting a dry skin and to sort out skin infections. Some people find that they have great results when applying palmarosa oil neat to the affected area of athlete's foot - but please keep in mind that we do not advocate the use of neat essential oils on the skin.

Palmarosa oil blends well with: geranium, bergamot, rosemary, lime and ylang-ylang.

CHAPTER FIFTY

PATCHOULI

Patchouli oil has a grounding and balancing effect on the emotions and banishes lethargy, while sharpening the wits, fighting depression and anxiety. It is also said to create an amorous atmosphere.

It is effective for fungal and bacterial infection and is of great help for insect bites. It could also be used as an insect repellant and is also used as a support for dealing with any substance addiction.

With its excellent diuretic properties, it is effective in fighting water retention and to break up cellulite, easing constipation and helping to reduce overweight. Furthermore, it has a great deodorizing action, and helps when feeling hot and bothered, while cooling down inflammations and assisting with wound healing. On the skin, this oil is one of the most active and is a superb tissue regenerator, which helps to stimulate the growth of new skin cells. In wound healing, it not only promotes faster healing, but also helps to prevent ugly scarring when the wound heals. Patchouli oil is very effective in sorting out rough, cracked and overly dehydrated skin and is used to treat acne, eczema, sores, ulcers, fungal infections as well as scalp disorders.

Summary

Patchouli oil has a beneficial effect on the skin, helps for infections and insect bites, water retention and can help with stress related problems and addictions.

Burners and vaporizers

In vapor therapy, patchouli oil can be used to fight anxiety and depression, while at the same time creating a very amorous atmosphere and acting as an insect repellent.

Blended massage oil or in the bath

As a blended massage oil or diluted in the bath, patchouli oil can help to fight depression, skin and scalp complaints, fungal infections, fluid retention, help to break down cellulite and also assists with constipation, overweight and dermatitis.

Neat

Patchouli oil can be applied neat with a cotton bud on insect bites.

Lotions and creams

In a lotion or cream, patchouli oil can be used for general skin care, as it has superb tissue regenerating properties, to help rejuvenate the skin and stimulate the formation of new skin cells, while fighting infections. It also speeds up healing, while preventing the wound forming ugly scars and is effective for acne, eczema, weeping sores, ulcers, slow healing wounds, scalp disorders, as well as other fungal infections, such as athlete's foot.

Patchouli oil blends well with: bergamot, clary sage, geranium, lavender and myrrh.

PEPPERMINT

Peppermint oil is excellent for mental fatigue and depression, refreshing the spirit and stimulating mental agility and improving concentration. It helps for apathy, shock, headache, migraine, nervous stress, vertigo and faintness and in general respiratory disorders, as well as dry coughs, sinus congestion, asthma, bronchitis, pneumonia, tuberculosis and cholera.

For the digestive system, peppermint oil is effective for a range of ailments, as it stimulates the gall bladder and the secretion of bile. It is used for colic, cramps, dyspepsia, spastic colon, flatulence and nausea and can relieve pain in cases of toothache, aching feet, rheumatism, neuralgia, muscular pains and painful periods.

On the skin, peppermint oil is used to relieve skin irritation and itchiness and also helps to reduce skin redness, where inflammation is present. It is used for dermatitis, acne, ringworm, scabies and pruritus and also relieves itching, sunburn and inflammation of the skin, while at the same time having a cooling action.

Summary

Peppermint oil can assist in nervous disorders and is dramatically effective in stimulating the mind and focusing concentration, for treating the respiratory tract, muscular aches and pains and for some skin problems.

Burners and vaporizers

In vapor therapy, peppermint oil can help to increase concentration and to stimulate the mind, as well as sorting out coughs, headaches, nausea and also has value as an insect repellant.

Blended oil or in the bath

As a blended massage oil or diluted in the bath, peppermint oil can assist with colic, cramps, back pain, inflamed bowel disorders, spastic colon, catarrh, colitis, circulation, constipation, coughs, diarrhea, sweaty and tired feet, flatulence, headaches, muscular pains, cramps and spasms, neuralgia, nausea, rheumatism and mental fatigue.Skin that is red, irritated and itchy, as well as other inflammatory conditions.

Mouthwash

A mouthwash with peppermint oil included can help with bad breath and gum infections.

Cream or lotion

When included in a cream or lotion, it will help to ease the sting of sunburn, reduce redness of inflamed skin, reduce itchiness and cools down the skin with its vasoconstrictor properties.

Peppermint oil blends well with: benzoin, eucalyptus, lavender, marjoram, lemon and rosemary.

CHAPTER FIFTY-TWO

PETITGRAIN

Petitgrain oil can help with nervous exhaustion and stress-related conditions and in particular anger and panic. It calms and soothes the mind, while relaxing the body, easing breathing, reducing rapid heart beat, relaxing muscle spasms and stomach pains.

It is great oil to use for convalescing after an illness and also for insomnia and helps to clear up a greasy skin, acne and excessive perspiration, while toning the skin.

Summary

Petitgrain oil helps with nervous problems, soothes aches and pains, and helps clear and tone the skin.

Burners and vaporizers

In vapor therapy, petitgrain oil can help with convalescence, anger, panic, depression and anxiety, calming irritation, while relaxing the body and boosting the conscious intellectual side of the mind.

Blended oil or in the bath

As a blended massage oil or diluted in the bath, it assist with convalescence, anxiety, irritability, anger, panic, tension, rapid heartbeat, pain and insomnia, while calming and relaxing the body and fighting skin blemishes.

Cream or lotion

When used in a cream or lotion, it is very useful to help clear up greasy skin and to release the congestion of such a skin, while at the same time helping to clear up acne, pimples and other skin blemishes.

Petitgrain oil blends well with: bergamot, lavender, palmarosa, geranium, rosewood and sandalwood.

CHAPTER FIFTY-THREE

PINE

Pine oil is most useful to relieve mental, physical and sexual fatigue, while having a cleansing and invigorating effect on an area and is great for vapor therapy in a sick room as it promotes healing.

It can be used for cuts and sores, scabies and lice and for excessive perspiration, while its warming properties help with rheumatism, arthritis, gout, muscular aches, pains and it can stimulate circulation.

Furthermore it can help in cases of bronchitis, asthma, catarrh, coughs, laryngitis, colds and flu. It eases breathlessness and sinusitis.

As a general kidney cleanser, it is effective with cystitis, prostate problems and urinary infections and can also help with nervous exhaustion, neuralgia and mental fatigue.

Summary

Pine oil can be useful in the treatment of the respiratory tract, for muscular aches and pains, and as a urinary cleanser.

Burners and vaporizers

In vapor therapy it can be used for asthma, colds, coughs, smokers cough, drowsiness, hangover and sinusitis.

Blended oil or in the bath

In a blended massage oil or diluted in the bath, it can be used for asthma, cellulite, colds, coughs, hangover, infections, rheumatism and sinusitis. Care should however be taken if you are prone to allergic reactions, and this oil may also irritate the mucus membranes.

Pine oil blends well with: cedarwood, eucalyptus, lavender, niaouli, rosemary and sage.

CHAPTER FIFTY-FOUR

ROSEMARY

Rosemary oil has a pronounced action on the brain and the central nervous system and is wonderful for clearing the mind and mental awareness, while having excellent brain stimulant properties, as well as improving memory. It helps with headaches, migraines, neuralgia, mental fatigue and nervous exhaustion and the antiseptic action of rosemary oil is especially suitable for intestinal infections and diarrhea, easing colitis, dyspepsia, flatulence, hepatic disorders and jaundice and relieving pain associated with rheumatism, arthritis, muscular pain and gout. It also helps for arteriosclerosis, palpitations, poor circulation and varicose veins. The diuretic properties of rosemary oil are useful with reducing water retention during menstruation, and also with obesity and cellulite. On the respiratory system, it is effective for asthma, bronchitis, catarrh, sinus and whooping cough. Because of its astringent action, it is also effective for countering sagging skin. Its stimulating action encourages hair growth. On the skin, it helps to ease congestion, puffiness and swelling and can also be used for acne, dermatitis and eczema, in hair care products, as it has a pronounced positive effect on the health of the hair and scalp. It increases the circulation to the scalp and is therefore also effective for promoting hair growth.

Summary

Rosemary oil is effective for mental fatigue, circulation problems, pain relief for the muscular system, decongests the respiratory tract and is a skin and hair booster.

Burners and vaporizers

In vapor therapy, rosemary oil can be helpful for congestion, alcohol over-indulgence, overwork, sinusitis and mental and physical tiredness. It furthermore stimulates the brain, improves memory and promotes clear thinking.

Blended massage oil or in the bath

As a blended massage oil or diluted in the bath, rosemary oil can assist with liver and gall problems, mucus congestion, muscular aches, cramps, pains and spasms, stiff neck, overwork, rheumatism, arthritis, colds, constipation, diarrhea, coughs, bronchitis, back pain, scalp disorders, sinusitis, mental fatigue and physical tiredness.

Cream or lotion

In a cream or lotion it is most beneficial for improving blood circulation and decongesting the skin.

Shampoo

When added to shampoo it not only increases the circulation to the scalp and thereby improving hair growth, but also acts as a general conditioner and tonic for the hair and scalp.

Rosemary oil blends well with: cedarwood, citronella, geranium, lavender, lemongrass, peppermint..

CHAPTER FIFTY-FIVE

ROSEWOOD

When feeling overburdened by the world, this oil will lift your spirits and have a balancing action effect on the mind and body. It is used with good results in reducing headaches, colds, coughs, fever and infections and is a boost for the immune system. Its aphrodisiac properties are useful to sort out sexual problems such as impotence and frigidity. It is an excellent oil to use in skincare, as it sorts out dull, dry and oily skin, while having a cell stimulant and tissue regenerating action on the skin which promotes rejuvenation of the skin.

Summary

Although rosewood oil does not have wide therapeutic properties, it has a place in aromatherapy and could help with the respiratory system, with sexual problems, with stress-related conditions and with great success for skin care.

Burners and vaporizers

In vapor therapy rosewood oil can help with colds, coughs, infections, headaches, nausea and stress-related problems, while lifting depression and helping to counter any sexual problems.

Blended massage oil or in the bath

As a blended massage oil or diluted in the bath, rosewood oil can help with colds, coughs, infections, headaches, fevers and nervous tension, as well as frigidity and impotence, while giving the skin a boost.

Lotions and creams

As part of a lotion or cream rosewood oil is most effective to stimulate the cells and regenerate tissue, therefore aiding rejuvenation of the skin and making it particularly attractive for use with more mature and wrinkled skin.

Rosewood oil blends well with: all citrus and floral oils.

CHAPTER FIFTY-SIX

SPEARMINT

When your mind is tired and in need of stimulating and upliftment, then spearmint oil is the one for you, and although it has very many properties in common to that of peppermint oil, it contains only small amounts of menthol and is far less harsh on the skin and ideal for use in children. It is very useful to deal with digestive problems including flatulence, constipation, diarrhea and nausea, as it relaxes the stomach muscles and also relieves hiccups. Furthermore, it helps with headaches, migraines, nervous strain, fatigue and stress, as well as for the respiratory tract; helping with asthma, bronchitis, catarrh and sinusitis.

On the skin it can relieve the itching of pruritus and helps with acne, dermatitis, congested skin and sore gums. For female health it can help to stem the flow of heavy periods and leucorrhoea and releases urine retention.

Summary

Spearmint oil can be effective for the digestive system, for the respiratory tract, for a tired mind and for skin problems.

Burners and vaporizers

In vapor therapy, spearmint oil can be used for vomiting, colic, flatulence, headaches, migraines, nervous conditions, asthma, bronchitis, sinusitis and catarrh.

Blended massage oil or in the bath

Used as blended massage oil or diluted in the bath, spearmint oil helps with headaches, migraines, stress, fatigue, sinusitis, asthma, bronchitis and nervous conditions and to relieve itching.

Cream or lotion

When spearmint oil is used in a cream or lotion it can help for itching - specially in cases of pruritus or when scabs have formed, decongesting the skin and to a lesser degree acne as well.

Spearmint oil blends well with: basil, eucalyptus, lavender, rosemary and jasmine.

CHAPTER FIFTY-SEVEN

TEA TREE

Tea tree oil is very important in the health of the immune system, as it acts as a immuno-stimulant and increases the body's ability to fight off any infections, while it also is used to revive the mind and body after shock.

The world over, this oil is used with great effectiveness to ward of infections of any kind, and it is active in all three varieties of infectious organisms: bacteri, fungi and viruses.

It can help with influenza, cold sores, catarrh, glandular fever and gingivitis. A course of massage with tea tree oil before an operation may help to fortify the body and reduce post-operative shock. Apart from the superb anti-infectious properties of tea tree oil, it is also most effective to help clear bronchial congestion, asthma, coughs, sinusitis, whooping cough and tuberculosis. On the genito-urinary system, it can be used to help clear vaginal thrush, cystitis and genital infections in general and on the skin, it clears abscesses, acne, burns, herpes, oily skin, athlete's foot, cold sores, blemishes, diaper rash, warts, sunburn and infected wounds, while fighting dandruff on the scalp.

Summary

Tea tree oil is one of the most powerful immune stimulant oils and helps fight infections of all kinds and helps clear the skin.

Burners and vaporizers

In vapor therapy, tea tree oil helps with colds, sinusitis, bronchitis and any other respiratory ailment and is also of use to help the mind cope after shock.

Blended massage oil or in the bath

As a blended massage oil or diluted in the bath, tea tree oil helps with all respiratory ailments, as well as arthritis, colds, dermatitis, skin infections, scalp disorders, sinusitis, viral infections, nettle rash, babies colds and coughs, bronchitis, as well as for sweaty feet.

In wash or applied neat

When it is added to the water for washing it has great value to treat abscesses, bed sores, acne, boils, lice, dandruff, wounds, as well as animal or human bites and can also be applied neat on problem areas with a cotton bud.

For lice - apply neat onto the scalp - leave for 40 minutes and wash the hair. This must be repeated every second day for twelve days.

Fungal outbreaks such as athlete's foot and nail infections (paronychia) as well as vaginal thrush and cradle cap can be treated with frequent direct application of a 2.5% dilution of tea tree oil.

Please remember that it is a powerful essential oil, and the neat application onto the skin must be done with care.

Mouthwash

Tea tree oil can be used as a mouthwash for gum infections, mouth ulcers, throat infections and tonsillitis,

Cream or lotion

When tea tree oil is blended into a cream or lotion and applied to the skin, it will help to clear up any fungal, bacterial as well as viral infections - and can therefore be used for a variety of problems - ranging from boils, abscesses, acne, bite wounds from animals and humans (although a medical practitioner must also be consulted), dandruff and other scalp disorders and is also effective to help sort out bed sores, diaper rash or any other rash.

Tea tree oil blends well with: cypress, eucalyptus, lavender, lemon, lemongrass, orange, rosemary and thyme.

THYME

Thyme oil strengthens the nerves, aids memory and concentration, can help with the feeling of exhaustion and combats depression, while it fortifies the lungs and helps with colds, coughs, asthma, laryngitis, sinusitis, catarrh, whooping cough, sore throats and tonsillitis.

Thyme oil is beneficial to boost the immune system and can help fight colds, flu, infectious diseases, chills and as a urinary antiseptic, it is very helpful for cystitis and urethritis.

The warming effect of this oil can help in cases of poor circulation, as well as for arthritis, rheumatism, gout, muscular aches and pains, sprains and sport injuries. It is also helpful for cellulite, anorexia, obesity and edema and in cases of scanty periods, leucorrhoea, and to speed up birth.

Summary

Thyme oil can assist with nervous complaints, respiratory problems, poor circulation and problems of the digestive system and the urinary tract.

Burners and vaporizers

In vapor therapy, thyme oil can be helpful with bronchitis, coughs, respiratory problems, sinusitis, mucus congestion and muscular aches and pains.

Blended oil

As a blended massage oil it can assist with arthritis, bronchitis, colds, flu, coughs, gout, bruises, eczema, mucus congestion, muscular aches and pains, obesity and rheumatism.

Mouthwash and gargle

Diluted as a mouthwash or as a gargle, thyme oil can help with gum infections and tonsillitis.

Neat application

Apply directly, or used neat, thyme oil could help with animal bites and boils but use with care, because of the possible of the risk of skin irritation.

Thyme oil blends well with: bergamot, grapefruit, lemon, lavender, rosemary and pine.

CHAPTER FIFTY-NINE

VETIVERT

Vetivert oil calms and soothes the mind and helps to dispel anger, hysteria and irritability. Neurotic behavior can also be reduced, as stress and tension is reduced. It revitalizes the body and helps with mental and physical exhaustion and is also used for general aches and pains, especially for rheumatism, arthritis and muscular pain, while relieving insomnia.

Summary

Vetiver oil has a calming and soothing effect on the nervous system and is helpful for muscular aches and pains, as well as having a positive effect on hormonal imbalance as well as relieving insomnia.

Burners and vaporizers

In vapor therapy, vetiver oil can be used for nervous complaints, dispelling hysteria, anger and irritability and also to relieve insomnia.

Blended massage oil or in the bath

In blended massage oil or diluted in the bath, vetiver oil can help with mental and physical exhaustion, nervous complaints, rheumatism and arthritic pain, insomnia as well as balancing the hormonal system and have a healing effect on the skin.

Cream or lotion

In a cream or lotion, it can be used to moisturize and nourish the skin and is specifically beneficial for dry, irritated and dehydrated skin. It is also helpful in reducing wrinkles and stretch marks and to improve the tone of slack skin, as well as helping wounds to heal.

Vetiver oil blends well with: benzoin, grapefruit, jasmine, lavender and ylang-ylang.

CHAPTER SIXTY

YLANG YLANG

Ylang-ylang oil has a euphoric and sedative effect on the nervous system and helps with anxiety, tension, shock, fear and panic while the aphrodisiac qualities is useful for impotence and frigidity.

It is particularly useful with rapid breathing and rapid heartbeat, it can also help with reducing high blood pressure and useful for intestinal infections.

On the skin, ylang-ylang oil has a soothing effect and its balancing action sorts out over-dry as well as overly-oily skin by balancing the secretion of sebum, and has a stimulating effect on the scalp which promotes more luxurious hair growth.

Summary

Ylang-ylang oil assist with problems such as high blood pressure, rapid breathing and heartbeat, nervous conditions, as well as impotence and frigidity.

Burners and vaporizers

In vapor therapy ylang-ylang oil can be helpful with anxiety, tension, shock, fear, panic, rapid breathing, rapid heartbeat, aphrodisiac, physical exhaustion, frigidity, impotence, insomnia, depression and stress.

Blended massage oil or in the bath

As a blended massage oil or diluted in the bath ylang-ylang will assist with physical exhaustion, insomnia, frigidity, impotence, depression, anxiety, nervous tension and stress while having a calming and aphrodisiac effect.

Cream or lotion

In a cream or lotion it is used to balance the production of sebum in the skin and thereby correcting and balancing overly-dry as well as overly-oily skin.

Ylang-ylang oil blends well with: bergamot, grapefruit, lavender and sandalwood.

CHAPTER SIXTY-ONE

ATTRIBUTES OF ESSENTIAL OILS

Achillea oil: Anti-inflammatory and hemostatic. Against hypertension, insomnia, and hemorrhoids. For gynecological diseases and neuralgia.

Angelica oil: Carminative and relaxing. For heart, respiratory and skin problems, anorexia, asthma, stomach ulcer, arthritis, and psoriasis.

Aniseed oil: Emmenagogu, antispasmodic and tonic. For menstruation, menopause's disease, dyspepsia, colitis, asthmatic bronchitis, and tachycardia.

Bassilicum oil: Tonic, refreshing, memory boosting, and insectifuge. For headaches, insomnia, depression, and nervous tension.

Balsam (Canada) oil: Antiseptic and relaxing. For asthma, bronchitis, dejection, and sore throat.

Balsam (Peru) oil: Anti-inflammatory, antiseptic, disinfectant. For wounds and stomach ulcers.

Balsam (Tolu) oil: Anti-inflammatory, antiseptic, excretory, and antitussive.

Benzoin oil: Excretory, calefacient, pulmonic and antiseptic. For acne, eczema, psoriasis, coughs, and bad blood circulation.

Bergamot oil: Refreshing, tonic, and calming. For stress, depression, insomnia, skin disorders, and digestive conditions.

Bitter Orange oil: Anti-inflammatory, antiseptic, styptic, antibacterial, fungicide, stomachic, and laxative. For stomach problems, enteric fermentation, constipation, acne, greasy skin and dyspepsia.

Black Pepper oil: Tonic to the digestive and respiratory system, toothache, bronchitis, rheumatisms, and sexual impotence.

Cajuput oil: Antiseptic, calefacient. For respiratory infections, varicose veins, and hemorrhoids.

Calendula oil: Anti-bleeding, anti-inflammatory, antiseptic, styptic, cicatrizant, and fungicide. For burns, wounds, eczema, greasy skin, skin inflammation and eruption, and against bites of insects.

Cardamon oil: Antiseptic, diuretic emmenagogue and dilatant for blood vessels. For digestive system, bronchitis and convulsion.

Carrotseed oil: Antiseptic, diuretic, dilatant for blood vessels and emmenagogue. For dermatitis, eczema, psoriasis, rheumatisms, arthritis, anemia, dyspepsia, anorexia, colics, and menstruation problems. It refreshes mature skin and relieves menstruation's pain.

Cedar oil: Insectifuge, antiseptic, calming, aphrodisiac, diuretic, styptic and fungicide. For acne, greasy skin, dandruff, hair loss, cough, bronchitis, cystitis, leucorrhoea, nervous tension, and genitals' itching. It helps hair regrowing and invigorates blood circulation.

Chamomile oil: Calming, refreshing, antiseptic, and emollient. For skin infections and stomach derangement.

Clove oil: Anti-infectious, antispasmodic, insectifuge, anti-fungicide, and tonic. For migraine, vertigo, stress, toothache, acne, wounds, burns, sprains, colic, seasickness, and dyspepsia.

Cinnamon oil: Antiseptic and antibacterial. For diarrhea, dyspepsia, bad blood circulation, and rheumatisms.

Citronella oil: Cardiotonic, antispasmodic, calming, insectifuge, and anti-louse. For rheumatisms, insomnia, stress, depression, otitis, arthritis, various colics, and pelvis pain.

Cistus oil: Styptic, relaxing, and calming. For elder skin and wrinkles.

Coriander oil: Calefacient, tonic and peptic. For stress and insomnia.

Cumin oil: Calefacient, tonic, and antiseptic. For dyspepsia, enteric convulsions and insomnia.

Cypress oil: Deodorant, styptic, diuretic, calming, and refreshing. For asthma, bronchitis, cellulitis, greasy skin, phlebitis, suppuration, gynecological and circulation problems.

Eucalyptus oil: Antiseptic, analgesic, pesticide. For flu, cold, sinusitis, laryngitis, cough, coxalgia, neuralgia, rheumatisms, and mental lucidity.

Fennel seed oil: Alleviative, anti-parasitic, purge, and against enteric fermentation. For all gynecological problems, water retention, and cystitis.

Fir (Black) oil: Antimicrobial, ejaculatory, and tonic. For rheumatisms, respiratory diseases, flu, cough, and stress.

Fir (Siberian) oil: Antiseptic and refreshing. For acne and bronchitis.

Frankincense oil: Refreshing, anti-inflammatory and immunizer. For asthma and bronchitis.

Ginger oil: Calefacient and peptic. For seasickness and various enteric diseases.

Grapefruit oil: Antioxidant and antispasmodic. For cellulitis, obesity, and urine retention.

Geranium oil: Circulation tonic, anti-aging, styptic, anti-cellulite, hemostatic and insectifuge. For stress, nervousness, urine retention, cellulitis, hemorrhoids, greasy skin, menopause, and gynecological problems.

Helichrysum oil: For wounds, burns, thrombosis, cirrhosis, and acne. It helps circulation and cholesterol problems.

Hyssop oil: Antiseptic. For blood dialysis, tonsillitis, and pneumonia.

Jasmine oil: Relaxing, calming, and aphrodisiac. For headache, menstrual period, dejection, and nervous fatigue.

Juniper oil: Anti-rheumatic, anti-toxic, emmenagogue, and tonic. For nervous strain, stress, gynecological diseases, arteriosclerosis, rheumatism, cellulite, and obesity.

Laurel oil: Insectifuge, antiseptic, diuretic, bactericide, fungicide, tonic, and refreshing. For rheumatisms, wounds, and hematoma.

Lavender oil: Analgesic, diuretic, styptic, refreshing, relaxing, and calming. For rheumatisms, muscle pain, colics, dyspepsia, depression, headaches, hypertension, insomnia, stress, and skin diseases.

Lemon oil: Refreshing, stimulating, antimicrobial, febrifuge, diuretic, antitoxic, hemostatic, and antiseptic. For rheumatisms, digestive and hepatic problems, greasy skin, arthritis, varicose veins, cellulite, obesity, brittle nails, flu, fever, sniffles, and dyspepsia.

Lemongrass oil: Analgesic, antidepressant, antiseptic and insecticidal. For digestive and hepatic problems.

Mandarin oil: Calming, antispasmodic, and anti-wrinkle. For acne, greasy skin, urine retention, obesity, dyspepsia, enteric problems, and insomnia.

Manuka oil: Antibacterial, fungicide and relaxant. For skin diseases, mycosis and psoriasis.

Marigold oil: For mycosis, respiratory infections, and enteric parasites.

Marjoram oil: Calefacient, corroborant, antispasmodic and muscle booster. For arthritis, rheumatisms, lumbago, colics, strains, constipation, cellulitis, dyspnoea, migraine, nervous tension, insomnia, and dizziness.

Mastic oil: Anti-inflammatory and antibiotic. For skin problems, arthritis, coxalgia, bronchitis, and urethritis.

May Chang oil: Antiseptic, deodorant, disinfectant, insecticidal stomachic, and calming. For acne, dermatitis, sudation, bloat, dyspepsia, heart arrhythmia, hypertension, and nervous tension.

Melissa oil: Antispasmodic, refreshing, and calming. For chronic cough, asthma, bronchitis, colics, menopause problems, stress, migraines, vertigo, insomnia, hysteria, and erethism.

Myrrh oil: Tonic and anti-aging. For dysentery, hemorrhoids, and hyperthyroidism.

Myrtle oil: For skin invigoration, greasy skin, hormone counterbalance, hemorrhoids, and ovary and thyroid problems.

Neroli oil: Refreshing, calming, and nervine. For parasites, hemorrhoids, exhaustion, and depression.

Niaouli oil: Antiseptic, anti-allergic against viruses. For otitis, laryngitis, and hormone problems.

Nutmeg oil: Peptic, calefacient, antioxidant and analgesic. For bloat, dyspepsia, seasickness, and muscle pain.

Orange oil: Calming, antispasmodic, and anti-wrinkle. For skincare, obesity, fluid retention, obesity, constipation, nervous tension, and stress.

Oregano oil: Antiseptic, deodorant, aphrodisiac, tonic, febrifuge, peptic, and pesticide. For massage, rheumatisms, cough, asthma, bronchitis, and cellulitis.

Patchouli oil: Relaxing and refreshing. For dry skin, acne, eczema. It helps nervous invigoration.

Petitgrain oil: Antiseptic, deodorant, peptic, and tonic. For acne, sudation, greasy skin and hair, dyspepsia, insomnia, and nervous exhaustion.

Pennyroyal oil: Tonic, insectifuge and emmenagogue.

Peppermint: Antiseptic, tonic, and anti-inflammatory. For coxalgia, dyspepsia, seasickness, fever, stress, and migraine.

Ravensara oil: Anti-infectious, nervine, and excretory. For insomnia and invigoration of chronic fatigue of the muscles.

Rose oil: Calming, relaxing, antidepressant, and anti-wrinkle. For chronic bronchitis, asthma, and sexual impotence.

Rosemary oil: Corroborant, emmenagogue, tonic, and antiseptic. For memory, and energy-boosting, muscle pain, rheumatisms, bad circulation. One of the best massage oils. It helps hair growth.

Rosewood oil: Anti-aging and tonic. For depression, fatigue, and respiratory infections.

Sage oil: Antiseptic. For cold, fever, stomach problems, cellulitis, obesity, herpes, and menstruation's problems. It is considered a decongestant for blood circulation.

Salvia Sclarea oil: Calming and antidepressant. For mental euphoria, menstruation problems, hemorrhoids, and nervous distress.

Sandalwood oil: Calming, anti-aging, and cardiotonic. Considered decongestant for vein and lymph.

Savory oil: Tonic, calefacient, aphrodisiac, antibiotic and anti-parasitic.

Tarragon oil: Calefacient and stimulating. For peptic and equilibration of the nervous system.

Tea Tree oil: Antiseptic and local anesthetic. For mycosis, enteric parasites, and various infections.

Thuya oil: Antiseptic, anti-inflammatory, and anti-bactericidal. It helps blood circulation.

Thyme oil: Antiseptic and antibiotic. For bronchitis and otitis.

Valerian oil: Soporific, hypotensive, and calming. For insomnia, migraine, nervous dyspepsia, and dandruff.

Vanilla oil: Aromatic, balsam and aphrodisiac.

Vetiver oil: Antiseptic, circulation tonic, and antispasmodic. For acne, arthritis, and rheumatism.

Vitex agnus castus oil: For gynecological and menopause problems, toothache and prostate. Used in hormonotherapy.

Ylang Ylang oil: Calming, antiseptic, aphrodisiac. For hypertension and skin diseases.

CHAPTER SIXTY-TWO

PSYCHOLOGICAL BENEFITS OF ESSENTIAL OILS

Balancing: basil, bergamot, frankincense, geranium, lavender, lemongrass.

Relaxing: cedarwood, clary sage, cypress, juniper, marjoram, myrrh, petitgarin, vetiver, ylang ylang.

Stimulating: black pepper, cardamom, cinnamon, clove, eucalyptus, fennel, ginger, lime, orange, palmarosa, patchouli, peppermint, pine, rosemary.

Antidepressant: basil, bergamot, clary sage, frankincense, geranium, lavender, lemon, lime, orange, palmarosa, patchouli, petitgrain, ylang ylang.

Aphrodisiac: cardamom, cedarwood, cinnamon, clary sage, clove, ginger, patchouli, rosemary, vetiver, ylang ylang.

Anaphrodisiac: camphor, marjoram.

CHAPTER SIXTY-THREE

ESSENTAIL OILS FOR HEALING

Potentially Helpful Essential Oils:

Wound Healing: Tea tree oil has antiseptic and antifungal properties that may help prevent infection.

Inflammation:L avender oil's anti-inflammatory properties may be helpful for conditions like muscle aches or pain.

Scarring: Some studies suggest frankincense oil may help reduce the appearance of scars. However, more research is needed.

Important Considerations:

Proper Wound Care: Clean and dress wounds appropriately to promote healing.

Medication: Follow your doctor's instructions regarding any prescribed medications.

Rest and Hydration: These are essential for the body's healing process.

Essential oils are potent and should be used with care. Here are some key safety precautions to remember:

Dilution is important: Essential oils are highly concentrated and must be diluted with a carrier oil like jojoba, almond, or coconut oil before applying them to your skin. A common ratio is 2-3 drops of essential oil per 1 tablespoon of carrier oil.

Sensitivity: Always do a patch test before using a new essential oil. Apply a small amount of the diluted blend to your inner forearm and wait 24 hours to see if there's any irritation.

Less is More: Start with a small amount of essential oil and gradually increase as needed.

Sensitive Areas: Avoid contact with eyes, mucous membranes, and damaged skin.

Pregnancy and Children: Consult a healthcare professional before using essential oils if pregnant, breastfeeding, or using them on children(below 9 years).

Remember: Consistency is key! Regularly using essential oil blends tailored to your skin type can offer noticeable benefits.

Essential oils should be used alongside medical advice, not as a replacement.

CHAPTER SIXTY-FOUR

ESSENTIAL OILS FOR FOOT PAIN

Potentially Helpful Essential Oils:

Peppermint oil: This oil contains menthol, which has a cooling effect and can help alleviate muscle aches and pains in the feet, including plantar fasciitis. It also has anti-inflammatory properties.

Lavender oil: Known for its calming properties, lavender oil may also help reduce pain and inflammation in the feet. Studies have shown it to be effective for pain relief after surgery.

Wintergreen oil: This oil is a powerful pain reliever but should be used with extreme caution due to its high salicylate content (similar to aspirin). It's best to dilute it heavily (1 drop to 100ml carrier oil) and avoid using it on large areas of skin or for long periods.

Cypress oil: This oil may help improve circulation in the feet, potentially reducing pain and discomfort caused by poor circulation.

How to Use Essential Oils for Foot Pain:

- Foot Soak: Add a few drops of diluted essential oil (peppermint, lavender, or cypress) to a warm foot soak for pain relief and improved circulation.
- Diluted Massage: Dilute essential oil with a carrier oil and massage it gently into your feet, focusing on painful areas.

Additional Tips for Foot Pain:

- Rest and Icing: Rest your feet and apply ice packs to reduce inflammation and pain.

- Proper Footwear: Ensure you wear supportive shoes that fit well.
- Stretching: Regularly stretching your feet and calves can help improve flexibility and reduce pain.
- Remember, consulting a doctor or podiatrist is crucial for addressing the root cause of your foot pain and getting the most effective treatment plan.

Caution:

- Dilution: Always dilute essential oils with a carrier oil before applying them to your skin.
- Patch test: Before using any new essential oil, do a patch test on your inner forearm to check for allergic reactions.
- Not a replacement for medical advice: If you have any underlying health conditions, are pregnant, or breastfeeding, consult a doctor before using essential oils.

CHAPTER SIXTY-FIVE

ESSENTIAL OILS FOR PAIN AND FATIGUE

For Pain:
Pain Relief and Inflammation:
Peppermint oil: This oil contains menthol, which has a cooling effect and can help alleviate muscle aches and pains. It also has anti-inflammatory properties.

Lavender oil: Known for its calming properties, lavender oil can also help reduce pain and inflammation. Studies have shown it to be effective for pain relief after surgery.

Clary sage oil: This oil may help with pain relief, particularly menstrual cramps. However, consult a doctor before using clary sage oil if you have any hormone-related conditions or are pregnant/breastfeeding.

Wintergreen oil: This oil is a powerful pain reliever but should be used with caution due to its salicylate content (similar to aspirin). It's best to dilute it heavily and avoid using it on large areas of skin.
For Fatigue:
Uplifting and Energizing Scents:
Rosemary oil: This oil is well-regarded for cognitive function and may help improve alertness and combat fatigue.

Lemon oil: With its uplifting and clarifying scent, lemon oil can help improve mood and energy levels.

Grapefruit oil: Similar to lemon oil, grapefruit oil has an invigorating aroma that can help combat fatigue and boost energy.

Using Essential Oils for Pain and Fatigue:

Diffuser: A diffuser is a good way to disperse the essential oil's scent throughout your space for inhalation.

Diluted Topical Application: Dilute a few drops of essential oil with a carrier oil like jojoba or almond oil. Apply a small amount to the affected area for pain relief (avoid open wounds) or to your wrists or temples for inhalation for fatigue.

Bath: Add a few drops of diluted essential oil to your bathwater for a relaxing and pain-relieving soak (for pain) or an invigorating and energizing bath (for fatigue).

Additional Tips:

- Pain: For pain relief, consider combining a pain-relieving oils like peppermint or lavender with a carrier oil and massaging it into the affected area. You can also use a warm compress soaked in diluted essential oil.
- Fatigue: Ensure you're getting enough sleep, eating a healthy diet, and staying hydrated. These lifestyle practices are crucial for managing fatigue.
- Remember, essential oils are complementary therapies and may not work for everyone. Be consistent with their use and consult a doctor if your pain or fatigue persists.

Caution:

- Dilution: Always dilute essential oils with a carrier oil before applying them to your skin.
- Patch test: Before using any new essential oil, do a patch test on your inner forearm to check for allergic reactions.
- Not a replacement for medical advice: If you have any underlying health conditions, are pregnant, or breastfeeding, consult a doctor before using essential oils.

CHAPTER SIXTY-SIX

ESSENTIAL OILS FOR HEADACHE

Potentially Helpful Essential Oils:

Lavender oil: Well-researched for its calming properties, lavender oil can help reduce tension headaches and promote relaxation. Studies have shown it to be effective in lowering anxiety and promoting feelings of calmness, which can be beneficial for headaches.

Peppermint oil: This oil contains menthol, which has a cooling and invigorating effect. It can help relieve muscle tension headaches and migraines by improving circulation.

Rosemary oil: This oil may help improve circulation and alleviate tension headaches.

How to Use Essential Oils for Headaches:

Inhalation: Add a few drops of diluted essential oil (lavender, peppermint, or rosemary) to a diffuser or steamer to inhale the scent.
Diluted Topical Application: Dilute essential oil with a carrier oil and apply a small amount to your temples, forehead, or back of your neck, avoiding your eyes.

Additional Tips for Headaches:

- Identify Triggers: Try to identify any potential triggers for your headaches, such as stress, certain foods, or lack of sleep. Addressing these triggers can help prevent future headaches.
- Hydration: Ensure you're drinking plenty of water throughout the day, as dehydration can contribute to headaches.
- Rest and Relaxation: Relaxation techniques like deep breathing exercises or meditation can help reduce tension and alleviate headaches.

Caution:

- Dilution: Always dilute essential oils with a carrier oil before applying them to your skin.
- Patch test: Before using any new essential oil, do a patch test on your inner forearm to check for allergic reactions.
- Not a replacement for medical advice: If you have any underlying health conditions, are pregnant, or breastfeeding, consult a doctor before using essential oils.

CHAPTER SIXTY-SEVEN

ESSENTIAL OILS FOR NERVOUS ISSUES

Essential oils can be a helpful tool for managing nervousness, anxiety, and promoting relaxation. However, it's important to remember that they are not a cure-all and should be used alongside other healthy lifestyle practices.

Calming and Stress-Reducing Scents:

Lavender oil: A well-researched and popular choice, lavender oil possesses calming and stress-reducing properties. Studies have shown it can be effective in lowering anxiety levels and promoting relaxation.

Cedarwood oil: This grounding oil can ease nervous tension and promote mental clarity, allowing you to feel more centered and manage anxiety better.

Clary sage oil: Known to regulate hormones, clary sage oil can be helpful in balancing mood swings and reducing anxiety, especially for women experiencing PMS. However, consult a doctor before using clary sage oil if you have any hormone-related conditions or are pregnant/breastfeeding.

Bergamot oil: Uplifting and mood-boosting, bergamot oil can help combat feelings of negativity, anxiety, and promote a more positive outlook.

Ylang-ylang oil: Mood-balancing properties and can ease feelings of anxiety and promote relaxation.

How to Use Essential Oils for Nervousness:

- Diffuser: An essential oil diffuser is a great way to fill the room with a calming scent.

- Diluted Topical Application: Dilute a few drops of essential oil with a carrier oil like jojoba or almond oil. Apply a small amount to your wrists or temples for inhalation.
- Bath: Add a few drops of diluted essential oil to your bathwater for a relaxing and stress-relieving soak.

Additional tips:

- Relaxation techniques: Practices like deep breathing exercises, meditation, and yoga can be very effective in reducing anxiety and promoting relaxation.
- Healthy lifestyle: Ensure you get enough sleep, maintain a balanced diet, and exercise regularly. These habits can significantly improve your overall well-being and reduce stress levels.
- Identify triggers: Pay attention to situations or events that trigger your nervousness and develop coping mechanisms to manage them effectively.
- Remember, consistency is key! Regularly using essential oils and incorporating healthy lifestyle practices can significantly reduce nervousness and promote a calmer state of mind.

Caution:

- Dilution: Always dilute essential oils with a carrier oil before applying them to your skin.
- Patch test: Before using any new essential oil, do a patch test on your inner forearm to check for allergic reactions.
- Not a replacement for medical advice: If you have any underlying health conditions, are pregnant, or breastfeeding, consult a doctor before using essential oils.

CHAPTER SIXTY-EIGHT

ESSENTIAL OILS FOR WORK RELATED STRESS

Calming and Focus-Enhancing Scents:
Lavender oil: Lavender oil's calming properties can help reduce anxiety and promote relaxation, creating a more peaceful work environment.

Cedarwood oil: This grounding oil can ease nervous tension and improve mental clarity, allowing you to better manage work pressure.

Vetiver oil: Known for its calming and centering properties, vetiver oil can help reduce anxiety and improve focus during demanding tasks.

Uplifting and Energizing Scents:
Rosemary oil: Well-regarded for memory and focus, rosemary oil can help improve alertness and concentration, potentially boosting your productivity.

Peppermint oil: This invigorating oil can help clear your mind, improve alertness, and enhance focus when facing work challenges.

Lemon oil: With its uplifting and clarifying scent, lemon oil can help improve concentration and mental clarity, allowing you to tackle work tasks more effectively.

Using Essential Oils for Work Stress:

- Diffuser: A diffuser is good to disperse the essential oil's scent throughout your workspace.

- Diluted Topical Application: Dilute a few drops of essential oil with a carrier oil like jojoba or almond oil. Apply a small amount to your wrists or temples for inhalation.
- Scent Inhaler: Create a DIY inhaler by adding a few drops of essential oil to a cotton ball and placing it in a nasal inhaler. Inhale occasionally throughout the day for a quick stress-relieving boost.

Caution:

- Dilution is key: Always dilute essential oils with a carrier oil before applying them to your skin.
- Start slow: Begin with a low dilution and gradually increase as needed to avoid overpowering yourself or colleagues in your workspace.
- Office environment: Be mindful of your work environment and colleagues. Some individuals may have sensitivities to essential oils. Consider diffusing for short bursts or using a personal inhaler.
- Remember, a holistic approach is key to managing work stress. In addition to essential oils, ensure you take breaks throughout the day, stay hydrated, and maintain a healthy work-life balance. If work stress is severe, consulting a therapist or counselor can provide valuable support.

ESSENTIAL OILS FOR PERIODS RELATED STRESS

Lavender oil: Lavender possesses calming and stress-reducing properties. It can help ease anxiety and promote relaxation, making you feel more centered during your period.

Clary sage oil: This oil is known to regulate hormones and can be helpful in balancing mood swings that sometimes occur during PMS. However, consult with a doctor before using clary sage oil if you have any hormone-related conditions or are pregnant/breastfeeding.

Bergamot oil: Uplifting and mood-boosting, bergamot oil can help combat feelings of negativity and promote a more positive outlook.

Ylang-ylang oil: Ylang Ylang oil has mood-balancing properties and can ease feelings of anxiety and promote relaxation.

How to Use Essential Oils for Period Stress:

- Diffuser: An essential oil diffuser is a great way to fill the room with a calming scent.
- Diluted Topical Application: Dilute a few drops of essential oil with a carrier oil like jojoba or almond oil. Apply a small amount to your wrists or temples for inhalation.
- Bath: Add a few drops of diluted essential oil to your bathwater for a relaxing and stress relieving soak.

Caution:

- Dilution: Always dilute essential oils with a carrier oil before applying them to your skin.
- Patch test: Before using any new essential oil, do a patch test on your inner forearm to check for allergic reactions.
- Not a replacement for medical advice: If you have any underlying health conditions, are pregnant, or breastfeeding, consult a doctor before using essential oils.

CHAPTER SEVENTY

ESSENTIAL OILS FOR ROMANCE

Classic Romantic Scents:

Rose Essential Oil: Rose absolute exudes a luxurious and romantic floral scent.

Jasmine Essential Oil: Jasmine absolute has a sweet, intoxicating aroma that is. mood-setting.

Ylang Ylang Essential Oil: This exotic oil has a sweet and floral aroma that's known to be relaxing and can heighten the senses.

Warming and Sensual Scents:

Sandalwood Essential Oil: Warm and woody, sandalwood oil has a grounding and sensual aroma that can be very inviting.

Patchouli Essential Oil: With its earthy, musky scent, patchouli oil is often considered a powerful aphrodisiac. However, its strong aroma can be polarizing, so use it sparingly.

Mood-Enhancing Scents:

Lavender Essential Oil: Lavender oil's calming and stress-reducing properties can create a relaxing and inviting atmosphere.

Bergamot Essential Oil: This citrus oil has a refreshing and uplifting aroma that can create a positive and inviting ambiance.

Blending Tips:

When using multiple essential oils, experiment to find a blend you enjoy. Start with a few drops of each oil and adjust based on your preference.

Consider using a diffuser to disperse the essential oils throughout the room. Alternatively, you can dilute them with a carrier oil and dab a small amount on your wrists or temples.

Remember, the most important aspect of creating a romantic atmosphere is to set the mood you and your partner enjoy.

Caution:

- Dilution: Always dilute essential oils with a carrier oil before applying them to your skin.
- Patch test: Before using any new essential oil, do a patch test on your inner forearm to check for allergic reactions.
- Not a replacement for medical advice: If you have any underlying health conditions, are pregnant, or breastfeeding, consult a doctor before using essential oils.

CHAPTER SEVENTY-ONE

ESSENTIAL OILS FOR RELAXATION

Soothing and Calming Scents:

Lavender oil: Lavender oil is well-known for its relaxing and stress-reducing properties. Studies have shown it can be effective in lowering anxiety and promoting feelings of calmness.

Chamomile oil: Chamomile oil possesses calming and sedative properties that can help ease anxiety and promote relaxation. It's also known for its sleep-promoting effects.

Bergamot oil: Uplifting and mood-boosting, bergamot oil can help combat feelings of negativity and anxiety, promoting a more relaxed and positive outlook.

Ylang-ylang oil: This oil has a calming and balancing effect on the nervous system, promoting relaxation and easing feelings of overwhelm.

Clary sage oil: Known to regulate hormones, clary sage oil can be helpful in balancing mood swings and reducing anxiety, especially for women experiencing PMS. However, consult a doctor before using clary sage oil if you have any hormone-related conditions or are pregnant/breastfeeding.

How to Use Essential Oils for Relaxation:

- Diffuser: A diffuser is a good way to disperse the essential oil's scent throughout your space for inhalation.
- Diluted Topical Application: Dilute a few drops of essential oil with a carrier oil like jojoba or almond oil. Apply a small amount to your wrists,

temples, or behind your ears for inhalation.

- Bath: Add a few drops of diluted essential oil to your bathwater for a relaxing and stress-relieving soak.

Enhancing Your Relaxation Routine:

- Combine with calming activities: Pair your essential oil use with activities that promote relaxation, such as reading, taking a warm bath, or listening to calming music.
- Create a relaxing atmosphere: Dim the lights, light candles, and ensure a comfortable temperature to create an inviting and peaceful space.
- Focus on your breath: Deep breathing exercises can be very effective in promoting relaxation. Combine them with inhaling the calming essential oil scents.
- For optimal relaxation, ensure you get enough sleep, maintain a healthy diet, and manage stress through other healthy habits. By incorporating essential oils and relaxation techniques into your routine, you can create a haven of peace and tranquility to unwind and de-stress.

Caution:

- Dilution: Always dilute essential oils with a carrier oil before applying them to your skin.
- Patch test: Before using any new essential oil, do a patch test on your inner forearm to check for allergic reactions.
- Not a replacement for medical advice: If you have any underlying health conditions, are pregnant, or breastfeeding, consult a doctor before using essential oils.

CHAPTER SEVENTY-TWO

ESSENTIAL OILS FOR MEDITATION

Promoting Relaxation and Focus:

Lavender oil: Lavender possesses calming and stress-reducing properties. It can help ease anxiety and promote relaxation, creating a more peaceful environment for meditation.

Frankincense oil: Known for its grounding and centering properties, frankincense oil can help quiet the mind and promote a sense of inner peace, ideal for meditation.

Sandalwood oil: This oil has a calming and slightly sweet aroma that can deepen your focus and enhance your meditation experience.

Cedarwood oil: This grounding oil can ease nervous tension and improve mental clarity, allowing you to better focus during meditation.

Uplifting and Alertness:

Rosemary oil: Well-regarded for memory and focus, rosemary oil can help improve alertness and concentration, potentially enhancing your meditation practice.

Peppermint oil: Invigorating and stimulating, peppermint oil can help clear your mind, improve alertness, and enhance focus during meditation.

Lemon oil: With its uplifting and clarifying scent, lemon oil can help improve concentration and mental clarity, allowing you to be more present during meditation.

Using Essential Oils for Meditation:

- Diffuser: An essential oil diffuser is a great way to disperse the oil's scent throughout your meditation space.
- Diluted Topical Application: Dilute a few drops of essential oil with a carrier oil like jojoba or almond oil. Apply a small amount to your wrists or temples for inhalation.
- Meditation Spray: Create a DIY spray by mixing a few drops of essential oil with water in a spray bottle. Spritz lightly around your meditation area (avoiding furniture) for a refreshing and focused environment.

Additional Tips:

- Set the mood: Dim the lights, light a candle, or play calming music to create a tranquil atmosphere for meditation.
- Comfort is key: Ensure you're comfortable in loose clothing and a supportive sitting position.
- Focus on your breath: Meditation often involves focusing on your breath to quiet the mind and achieve a state of relaxation.

Caution:

- Dilution: Always dilute essential oils with a carrier oil before applying them to your skin.
- Patch test: Before using any new essential oil, do a patch test on your inner forearm to check for allergic reactions.
- Not a replacement for medical advice: If you have any underlying health conditions, are pregnant, or breastfeeding, consult a doctor before using essential oils.

By incorporating essential oils into your meditation routine, you can create a more immersive and personalized experience that promotes relaxation, focus, and inner peace.

CHAPTER SEVENTY-THREE

ESSENTIAL OILS FOR STUDENTS

Enhancing Focus and Memory:

Rosemary oil: This oil is a memory booster and concentration enhancer. Studies suggest it may be just as effective as some conventional medications for improving cognitive function.

Peppermint oil: Known for its invigorating aroma, peppermint oil can help clear your mind, improve alertness, and enhance focus during studying.

Lemon oil: This citrus oil has an uplifting and clarifying scent that can help improve concentration and mental clarity.

Promoting Relaxation and Reducing Stress:

Lavender oil: Lavender oil's calming properties can help reduce anxiety and promote relaxation, creating a more focused study environment.

Cedarwood oil: This grounding oil can help ease nervous tension and promote mental clarity, allowing you to better absorb information.

Vetiver oil: Known for its calming and centering properties, vetiver oil can help reduce anxiety and improve focus during studying.

Using Essential Oils for Studying:

- Diffuser: An essential oil diffuser is a good way to disperse the oil's scent throughout your study space.
- Diluted Topical Application: Dilute a few drops of essential oil with a carrier oil like jojoba or almond oil. Apply a small amount to your wrists

or temples for inhalation.
- Study Spray: Create a DIY study spray by mixing a few drops of essential oil with water in a spray bottle. Spritz lightly around your study area (avoiding furniture) for a refreshing and focused environment.

Caution:

- Dilution: Always dilute essential oils with a carrier oil before applying them to your skin.
- Patch test: Before using any new essential oil, do a patch test on your inner forearm to check for allergic reactions.
- Not a replacement for medical advice: If you have any underlying health conditions, are pregnant, or breastfeeding, consult a doctor before using essential oils.

CHAPTER SEVENTY-FOUR

ESSENTIAL OILS FOR SKINCARE

Popular Essential Oils for Skincare:
Dry Skin:
Lavender oil: Lavender oil can help soothe dry and irritated skin.

Rosehip oil: Rich in vitamin A, rosehip oil helps promote hydration and cell regeneration, beneficial for dry skin. (Rosehip oil is a carrier oil, hence can be used on its own)
Geranium oil: Geranium oil helps balance sebum production, potentially aiding dry skin that lacks natural oils.
Tea tree oil: Tea tree oil's antibacterial properties can help combat blemishes and regulate oil production in oily skin.

Jojoba oil: Similar to sebum (skin's natural oil), jojoba oil can help regulate oil production and balance oily skin. (Jojoba oil is a carrier oil, hence can be used on its own)
Grapefruit oil: This oil has astringent properties that can help tighten pores and reduce excess oil.

Mature Skin:
Frankincense oil: Known for its regenerative properties, frankincense oil may help reduce the appearance of wrinkles and fine lines.

Carrot seed oil: Rich in antioxidants, carrot seed oil can help improve skin elasticity and reduce the appearance of wrinkles.

Helichrysum oil: This oil has anti-inflammatory properties that may help soothe and rejuvenate mature skin.

Caution:

- Dilution: Essential oils are highly concentrated and must be diluted with a carrier oil like jojoba, almond, or coconut oil before applying them to your skin. A common ratio is 2-3 drops of essential oil per 1 tablespoon of carrier oil.
- Sensitivity: Always do a patch test before using a new essential oil. Apply a small amount of the diluted blend to your inner forearm and wait 24 hours to see if there's any irritation.
- Sun Sensitivity: Some essential oils like citrus oils (lemon, grapefruit) can increase sun sensitivity. Avoid using them on exposed skin before sun exposure.
- Pregnancy and Breastfeeding: Consult a healthcare professional before using essential oils if you're pregnant or breastfeeding.
- Remember: Consistency is key! Regularly using essential oil blends tailored to your skin type can offer noticeable benefits.
- However, for any severe skin concerns, consult a dermatologist for personalized advice.

CHAPTER SEVENTY-FIVE

ESSENTIAL OIL FOR HAIRCARE

For hair growth:

Rosemary oil is a popular choice for hair growth. It can be combined with other oils like lavender, cedarwood, and thyme for a more complex scent.

Cedarwood essential oil is good for dandruff related issues.

Tea tree oil has antifungal and antibacterial properties that can help to combat dandruff. It can be mixed with a carrier oil like jojoba or coconut oil and massaged into the scalp.

Ylang ylang oil can help to balance sebum production and add moisture to dry hair. It can be mixed with a carrier oil like almond or avocado oil.

Choose the right essential oil blend based on your specific hair concerns. For example, rosemary for thinning hair, lavender/ylang ylang for dry hair, or tea tree for oily hair.

Application methods:

Scalp massage: Mix your chosen blend with carrier oil and massage it into your scalp for improved circulation and scalp health.

Hair mask: Add a few drops of the blend to your regular conditioner or hair mask for deep conditioning benefits.

Steam treatment: Add a few drops of the blend to a bowl of hot water (not boiling) and inhale the steam with a towel over your head for improved scalp health and relaxation.

Caution:

- Dilution: Always dilute essential oils with a carrier oil before applying them to your skin.

- Patch test: Before using any new essential oil, do a patch test on your inner forearm to check for allergic reactions.
- Not a replacement for medical advice: If you have any underlying health conditions, are pregnant, or breastfeeding, consult a doctor before using essential oils.

CHAPTER SEVENTY-SIX

ESSENTIAL OILS FOR PREMATURE HAIR FALL

Scalp Stimulation:

Rosemary oil: A well-researched oil known to promote hair growth by stimulating blood circulation to the scalp. It might be as effective as minoxidil for hair growth.

Cedarwood oil: This oil has scalp-soothing properties and may stimulate hair follicles, encouraging healthy growth. It may also help regulate sebum production on the scalp.

Tea tree oil: This oil has antifungal and antibacterial properties that can help combat dandruff and other scalp conditions that can contribute to hair loss.

Lavender oil: Known for its calming properties, lavender oil can help reduce scalp inflammation which can be a factor in hair loss.

Here's a potential DIY hair mask recipe you can try (twice a week):

Mix 2 tablespoons of carrier oil (like jojoba or coconut) with 2 drops each of rosemary and cedarwood essential oil.

Massage the blend gently into your scalp for a few minutes.

Leave it on for 20-30 minutes before washing your hair with a gentle shampoo.

Additional Tips:

Manage stress: Stress can be a major contributor to hair loss. Relaxation techniques like yoga or meditation can be beneficial.

Diet and nutrition: Ensure a balanced diet rich in vitamins and minerals for healthy hair growth. Biotin, iron, and vitamin D are particularly important.

Gentle hair care: Avoid harsh shampoos, tight hairstyles, and excessive heat styling which can damage hair follicles and contribute to hair loss.

Remember, consistency is key. It may take some time to see results, and essential oils should be used alongside a healthy lifestyle for optimal hair health. If your hair loss is severe or persistent, it's always best to consult a dermatologist to determine the underlying cause.

Caution:

- Dilution: Always dilute essential oils with a carrier oil before applying them to your skin.
- Patch test: Before using any new essential oil, do a patch test on your inner forearm to check for allergic reactions.
- Not a replacement for medical advice: If you have any underlying health conditions, are pregnant, or breastfeeding, consult a doctor before using essential oils.

CHAPTER SEVENTY-SEVEN

ESSENTIAL OILS FOR GREY HAIR

While there's no scientific evidence that essential oils definitively reverse grey hair, some essential oils have properties that may be helpful for overall hair health and potentially contribute to a darker appearance.

Rosemary oil: This oil is a popular choice for hair growth and pigmentation. Studies suggest it may be as effective as minoxidil (a common hair loss treatment) in promoting hair growth.

Sage oil: Sage oil boasts antioxidant properties that can neutralize free radicals which contribute to hair greying. It also has astringent properties for regulating oil production, promoting a balanced scalp.

Cedarwood oil: This oil has scalp-soothing properties and may stimulate hair follicles, encouraging healthy growth.

Lavender oil: While not specifically known for darkening hair, lavender oil promotes overall hair health and has calming properties for the scalp.

A scalp massage blend:

Combine 2-3 drops each of rosemary oil, cedarwood oil, and a few drops of lavender oil with 1 tablespoon of carrier oil.

Massage the blend gently into your scalp for a few minutes.

Leave it on for 20-30 minutes before washing your hair.

Remember, maintaining healthy hair habits like a balanced diet and managing stress can also contribute to overall hair health. It's always best to consult with a dermatologist if you have concerns about hair loss or premature greying.

Caution:

• Dilution: Always dilute essential oils with a carrier oil before applying them to your skin.

- Patch test: Before using any new essential oil, do a patch test on your inner forearm to check for allergic reactions.
- Not a replacement for medical advice: If you have any underlying health conditions, are pregnant, or breastfeeding, consult a doctor before using essential oils.

CHAPTER SEVENTY-EIGHT

ESSENTIAL OILS AND SPORTS

Essential oils have become increasingly popular among athletes for their potential benefits before, during, and after workouts. Here's a breakdown of how essential oils can be used in sports:

Benefits:

Reduced Muscle Soreness and Inflammation: Certain essential oils possess anti-inflammatory and analgesic properties. Common choices include wintergreen, peppermint, and clove, which can be diluted and massaged onto muscles to help ease soreness and inflammation.

Improved Recovery: Essential oils may promote blood circulation and lymphatic drainage, aiding the body's natural recovery process. Cypress, juniper, and rosemary are some examples used in massage blends.

Enhanced Focus and Motivation: Inhaling specific essential oils like rosemary, peppermint, and lemon can stimulate the mind and improve concentration. Diffusing these oils before a workout can be helpful.

Reduced Stress and Anxiety: Pre-competition jitters are common. Lavender, chamomile, and bergamot are known for their calming and relaxing effects, which can be beneficial for athletes experiencing anxiety.

How to Use:

Diffusion: Diffusing essential oils into the air using a diffuser is a good way to inhale the beneficial compounds.

Topical Application: Essential oils must be diluted in a carrier oil like almond oil or jojoba oil before applying them to the skin for massage.

Bath Soaks: Adding a few drops of essential oils to a warm bath can be a relaxing way to soothe sore muscles after exercise.

Important Considerations:

Research: While there's anecdotal evidence for the benefits of essential oils in sports, scientific research is still ongoing.

Dilution: Essential oils are concentrated and can irritate the skin. Always dilute them properly before topical application.

Potential Allergic Reactions: Conduct a patch test before using any new essential oil to check for allergic reactions.

Not a Replacement for Medical Advice: Essential oils should not be used as a substitute for professional medical advice.

Remember: Consult a healthcare professional or a certified aromatherapist before using essential oils, especially if you have any underlying health conditions or are pregnant or breastfeeding.

CHAPTER SEVENTY-NINE

ESSENTIAL OILS AS AN INSECT REPELLANT

Citronella oil: This is a classic insect repellent, often used in outdoor candles and torches. It's effective against mosquitoes, flies, and maybe some other insects.

Lemon eucalyptus oil: This oil is approved by the CDC as an effective mosquito repellent. It provides protection similar to DEET, but for a shorter duration.

Lavender oil: This versatile oil can repel mosquitoes, flies, fleas, and even ticks. It's known for its calming scent as well.

Tea tree oil: Tea tree oil has shown effectiveness against mosquitoes and other insects. However, it can be irritating to the skin, so dilution is crucial.

Peppermint oil: This oil repels a wide range of insects, including mosquitoes, ants, and spiders. It has a strong invigorating scent.

Effectiveness: While these essential oils offer some protection, they generally don't last as long as commercial repellents containing DEET. Reapplication is more frequent.

Tips for using essential oils as insect repellents:

Diffuser: Diffuse the essential oils in a diffuser to create a bug-repellent zone in an outdoor area.

Spray: Mix diluted essential oils with water in a spray bottle and apply to clothing (not directly onto skin unless heavily diluted).

Wipes: Create wipes by soaking cotton balls or cloths in a diluted essential oil solution.

Remember: While essential oils can provide some defense against insects, they may not be a perfect solution.

DEET (chemical name, N,N-diethyl-meta-toluamide) is the active ingredient in many repellent products. It is widely used to repel biting pests such as mosquitoes and ticks.

CHAPTER EIGHTY

ESSENTIAL OILS AS PESTICIDE

Pros:

Safer for Humans and Pets: Generally, essential oils are considered less toxic to humans and pets compared to synthetic pesticides.

Natural and Renewable: Essential oils are derived from plants and are considered a renewable resource. Multiple Pest Control: Certain essential oils can repel or kill a broad spectrum of insects, mites, and even some fungi.

Organic Suitability: Since they come from natural sources, some essential oils are suitable for organic farming.

Cons:

Limited Residual Effect: Unlike synthetic pesticides, essential oils typically have a shorter window of repellency or killing power. More frequent reapplication is needed.

Specificity: While some essential oils target a range of pests, they may not be effective against all types.

Break Down Quickly: Sunlight and rain can degrade essential oils quickly, reducing their effectiveness outdoors.

Potency Variations: The potency of essential oils can vary depending on plant source, extraction method, and storage conditions.

Essential oils used for pest control:

Neem oil: Repels and kills a variety of insects, mites, and even fungus.

Peppermint oil: Repels ants, spiders, and some beetles.

Lavender oil: Repels flies, moths, and mosquitoes.

Tea tree oil: Has insecticidal properties and may repel some insects.

Citronella oil: A classic mosquito repellent, also effective against some other flying insects.

While essential oils offer an eco-friendly approach to pest control, they may not be a complete replacement for synthetic pesticides.

Due to their short residual effect, repeated application of the solution is required in comparison to synthetic pesticides.

CHAPTER EIGHTY-ONE

ESSENTIAL OILS FOR PETCARE

generally animals are averse to strong odour

Safe vs. Toxic Essential Oils for Pets:

Cats: Cats are especially sensitive to essential oils because they lack the enzyme needed to properly metabolize essential oils. Many essential oils are toxic to cats and should never be used around them.

Dogs: Generally, dogs are less sensitive to essential oils than cats.

Safe essential oils for pets when used properly:

Lavender Oil: Lavender oil is known for its calming properties and can be used to help pets relax. It may also have mild antibacterial and anti-inflammatory effects.

Chamomile Oil: Chamomile oil is another calming oil that can help reduce anxiety in pets. It may also be soothing for skin irritations when diluted properly.

Frankincense Oil: Frankincense oil is often used to promote relaxation and reduce stress. It may also have anti-inflammatory properties.

Cedarwood Oil: Cedarwood oil can be helpful for repelling fleas and ticks when diluted and used properly. It has a woody aroma that some pets find it pleasant.

Peppermint Oil (in moderation): Peppermint oil can be used sparingly to help repel insects, but it should be heavily diluted and used with caution around pets, especially cats, as it can be irritating to their respiratory system.

Ginger Oil: Ginger oil may help alleviate nausea and motion sickness in pets when used in moderation and properly diluted.

Frankincense: Known for anti-inflammatory properties.

Toxic essential oils to pets:

Tea Tree Oil: Tea tree oil, also known as melaleuca oil, is toxic to pets, especially cats and small dogs. It can cause symptoms such as drooling, vomiting, difficulty walking, tremors, and even liver damage when ingested in large quantities.

Pennyroyal Oil: Pennyroyal oil is highly toxic to pets, particularly cats, and can cause severe liver damage and even death if ingested.

Pine Oil: Pine oil, commonly used in cleaning products and some aromatherapy blends, can be toxic to pets, especially if ingested in large amounts. It can cause symptoms such as vomiting, diarrhea, and lethargy.

Wintergreen Oil: Wintergreen oil contains methyl salicylate, which is toxic to pets if ingested. It can cause symptoms such as vomiting, diarrhea, rapid breathing, and even organ damage.

Cinnamon Oil: Cinnamon oil can irritate a pet's skin and mucous membranes, and if ingested in large amounts, it can cause symptoms such as vomiting, diarrhea, low blood sugar, and liver disease.

Citrus Oil: Citrus oils, including lemon, orange, and grapefruit, can cause skin irritation and gastrointestinal upset in pets. Additionally, the high concentration of limonene in citrus oils can be toxic if ingested in large amounts.

Eucalyptus Oil: Eucalyptus oil can be toxic to pets, particularly if ingested. It can cause symptoms such as drooling, vomiting, diarrhea, weakness, and difficulty breathing.

Ylang Ylang Oil: Ylang ylang oil can cause skin irritation and gastrointestinal upset in pets if ingested or applied undiluted to the skin.

Tips:

Consult a VET: Before using any essential oil around your pet, it's crucial to consult with a VET. They can provide guidance on which oils are safe for your specific pet and how to use them appropriately.

Dilution: If you're using essential oils around pets, always dilute them properly. Even oils that are considered safe for pets can be harmful if used undiluted.

Observation: When introducing essential oils to your pet, observe their reactions closely. If you notice any signs of discomfort or adverse effects, stop using the oil immediately and consult your vet.

Diffusion: If you're using essential oils in a diffuser, make sure your pet has the option to leave the room if they want to. Also, ensure that the diffuser is placed in an area where your pet cannot knock it over.

Sensitive Animals: Some pets, such as cats, are more sensitive to certain essential oils than others. Be especially cautious when using oils around these animals.

Brushing: Regular brushing can help remove dirt, dander, and pests, promoting healthy skin and coat.

Oatmeal baths: Oatmeal baths can soothe itchy skin.

VET consultation: If your pet has a skin condition, anxiety issue, or other concern, a veterinarian can recommend safe and effective solutions.

CHAPTER EIGHTY-TWO

ESSENTIAL OILS and GEM STONES

this is an esoteric subject, no proof available, consider it as suggestions and act accordingly

1. Amethyst and Lavender: Amethyst is often associated with promoting spiritual awareness and intuition, while lavender essential oil is known for its calming and relaxing properties. Together, they may create a soothing atmosphere conducive to meditation or deep relaxation.

2. Citrine and Citrus: Citrine is believed to bring positivity, abundance, and joy, while citrus essential oils such as lemon, orange, or grapefruit are uplifting and energizing. This combination may help boost mood and motivation, making it great for starting the day on a positive note.

3. Rose Quartz and Rose: Rose quartz is associated with love, compassion, and emotional healing, while rose essential oil is known for its floral aroma and ability to promote feelings of self-love and acceptance. Together, they can create a nurturing environment for fostering love and emotional well-being.

4. Lapis Lazuli and Frankincense: Lapis lazuli is often linked to enhancing communication, wisdom, and inner truth, while frankincense essential oil has grounding and spiritually uplifting properties. This combination may support clarity of mind, deepening meditation practices, or fostering introspection.

5. Black Tourmaline and Patchouli: Black tourmaline is believed to provide protection from negative energies and promote grounding, while patchouli essential oil has earthy and grounding qualities. Together, they can create a sense of stability and protection, making this combination beneficial for grounding practices or creating a sense of safety and security.

Remember, the effectiveness of these combinations can vary from person to person, and it's essential to trust your intuition and choose combinations that resonate with you personally.

Experiment with different pairings, and pay attention to how they make you feel to discover what works best for you.

CHAPTER EIGHTY-THREE

ESSENTIAL OILS AND GEM STONES AND BIRTH STAR

this is an esoteric subject, no proof available, consider it as suggestions and act accordingly

Combining essential oils with your birthstone can create a personalized and meaningful blend. Here are some suggestions based on birth months and their corresponding birthstones:

1. January (Garnet): Try blending grounding essential oils like cedarwood or vetiver with uplifting citrus oils such as bergamot or orange. This combination can help balance the energy of garnet, promoting stability and vitality.

2. February (Amethyst): Pair the calming scent of lavender essential oil with the spiritually uplifting aroma of frankincense. This blend can enhance the intuitive and spiritual qualities associated with amethyst, promoting relaxation and clarity of mind.

3. March (Aquamarine): Combine the fresh, aquatic scent of eucalyptus with the soothing aroma of chamomile. This blend can complement the tranquil and cleansing properties of aquamarine, promoting emotional balance and clarity.

4. April (Diamond): Blend energizing essential oils like peppermint or lemon with floral notes such as jasmine or rose. This combination can enhance the clarity and vitality associated with diamond, promoting focus and inspiration.

5. May (Emerald): Pair the grounding scent of patchouli with the refreshing aroma of spearmint. This blend can harmonize with the rejuvenating and heart-opening properties of emerald, promoting inner peace and vitality.

6. June (Pearl, Alexandrite, Moonstone): Combine the soothing scent of ylang-ylang with the balancing aroma of geranium. This blend can resonate

with the nurturing and emotional healing properties associated with pearl, alexandrite, or moonstone, promoting self-love and emotional harmony.

7. July (Ruby): Blend spicy essential oils like cinnamon or ginger with floral notes such as rose or geranium. This combination can complement the passionate and energizing qualities of ruby, promoting confidence and vitality.

8. August (Peridot): Pair the uplifting scent of grapefruit with the grounding aroma of cedarwood. This blend can harmonize with the cleansing and revitalizing properties of peridot, promoting clarity and emotional well-being.

9. September (Sapphire): Combine the calming scent of lavender with the clarifying aroma of lemon. This blend can resonate with the wisdom and intuition associated with sapphire, promoting mental clarity and spiritual insight.

10. October (Opal, Tourmaline): Blend earthy essential oils like sandalwood or patchouli with floral notes such as rose or jasmine. This combination can enhance the emotional healing and balance associated with opal or tourmaline, promoting inner peace and harmony.

11. November (Topaz, Citrine): Pair the uplifting scent of bergamot with the grounding aroma of vetiver. This blend can complement the warmth and abundance associated with topaz or citrine, promoting positivity and vitality.

12. December (Turquoise, Tanzanite, Zircon): Combine the calming scent of chamomile with the soothing aroma of lavender. This blend can resonate with the protective and healing properties of turquoise, tanzanite, or zircon, promoting relaxation and emotional balance.

These combinations can serve as a starting point for creating personalized blends that align with your birthstone and intentions.

Experiment with different essential oils and adjust the ratios based on your preferences and sensitivities.

CHAPTER EIGHTY-FOUR

ESSENTIAL OILS AND CHAKRAS(ENERGY CENTRES)

this is an esoteric subject, no proof available, consider it as suggestions and act accordingly

Essential oils and their corresponding chakras:

- **Root Chakra (Muladhara):**

  Location: Base of the spine.
  Associated with: Security, stability, survival.
  Essential oils: Cedarwood, Patchouli, Vetiver.
  These grounding oils help to promote feelings of safety and security.

- **Sacral Chakra (Swadhisthana):**

  Location: Lower abdomen, below the navel.
  Associated with: Creativity, emotions, sexuality.
  Essential oils: Orange, Ylang-Ylang, Sandalwood.
  These oils help to enhance creativity, sensuality, and emotional balance.

- **Solar Plexus Chakra (Manipura):**

  Location: Upper abdomen, around the stomach area.
  Associated with: Confidence, personal power, self-esteem.
  Essential oils: Lemon, Ginger, Bergamot.
  These oils help to boost confidence, increase energy, and promote a sense of empowerment.

- **Heart Chakra (Anahata):**

Location: Center of the chest, near the heart.
Associated with: Love, compassion, forgiveness.
Essential oils: Rose, Lavender, Jasmine.
These oils help to open the heart, promote love and compassion, and facilitate emotional healing.

- **Throat Chakra (Vishuddha):**

Location: Throat area.
Associated with: Communication, self-expression, truth.
Essential oils: Peppermint, Eucalyptus, Chamomile.
These oils help to clear communication blockages, enhance self-expression, and promote clarity of speech.

- **Third Eye Chakra (Ajna):**

Location: Forehead, between the eyebrows.
Associated with: Intuition, insight, imagination.
Essential oils: Lavender, Frankincense, Clary Sage.
These oils help to enhance intuition, promote clarity of thought, and stimulate the imagination.

- **Crown Chakra (Sahasrara):**

Location: Top of the head.
Associated with: Spiritual connection, enlightenment, higher consciousness.
Essential oils: Frankincense, Sandalwood, Myrrh.
These oils help to deepen spiritual awareness, facilitate meditation, and connect with higher states of consciousness.

When using essential oils for chakra balancing, it's essential to consider your individual needs and preferences.

ESSENTIAL OILS IN VAASTU(INDIAN FENG SHUI)

this is an esoteric subject, no proof available, consider it as suggestions and act accordingly

ESSENTIAL OILS FOR ALL THE 8 DIRECTIONS

1. North: Associated with career, opportunities, and abundance.
- Peppermint: Enhances mental clarity and focus.
- Cedarwood: Grounding and promotes stability.
- Bergamot: Uplifting and fosters positivity and abundance.

2. Northeast: Linked to wisdom, knowledge, and spiritual growth.
- Frankincense: Promotes spiritual awareness and introspection.
- Lavender: Calming and aids in relaxation and meditation.
- Sandalwood: Grounding and enhances spiritual connection.

3. East: Represents health, vitality, and new beginnings.
- Lemon: Refreshing and promotes clarity and vitality.
- Eucalyptus: Invigorating and revitalizes the mind and body.
- Rosemary: Stimulating and enhances mental clarity and focus.

4. Southeast: Connected to wealth, prosperity, and abundance.
- Orange: Uplifting and fosters joy and positivity.
- Ginger: Energizing and promotes abundance and prosperity.
- Patchouli: Grounding and enhances stability and growth.

5. South: Associated with fame, recognition, and social interactions.
- Jasmine: Boosts confidence and self-esteem.
- Ylang-Ylang: Sensual and enhances charisma and social interactions.
- Basil: Energizing and promotes clarity and communication.

6. Southwest: Linked to relationships, emotional well-being, and creativity.
- Lavender: Calming and aids in relaxation and emotional balance.
- Chamomile: Soothing and promotes emotional harmony.

- Rose: Enhances love, compassion, and connection.

7. West: Represents partnerships, creativity, and inspiration.

- Rosemary: Stimulating and enhances creativity and inspiration.

- Geranium: Balancing and fosters emotional harmony and creativity.

- Sandalwood: Grounding and enhances stability and creativity.

8. Northwest: Connected to travel, helpful people, and support.

- Lemongrass: Uplifting and promotes optimism and positivity.

- Clary Sage: Balancing and enhances intuition and clarity.

- Cedarwood: Grounding and fosters stability and support.

ESSENTIAL OILS FOR THE CENTRE OF PROPERTY

1. Frankincense: This oil is often used for spiritual connection and grounding.

2. Lavender: This oil can promote a peaceful atmosphere and help balance emotions.

3. Sandalwood: Ideal for promoting harmony in the center of your space.

4. Patchouli: Great choice for fostering stability and balance in the center of your space.

5. Rosemary: Good option for promoting focus and balance in the center of your space.

These essential oils can be used individually or blended together to create a customized aroma that resonates with you and supports the overall energy of your space.

These essential oils can be used in diffusers or room sprays.

Experiment with different combinations and observe how they influence the energy and atmosphere within each direction of your space.

CHAPTER EIGHTY-SIX

CARRIER OILS

The term carrier oil is generally limited to use within the practice of aromatherapy. In natural skincare, carrier oils are typically referred to as vegetable oils, fixed oils, or base oils.

A carrier oil is a vegetable oil derived from the fatty portion of a plant, usually from the seeds, kernels, or nuts.

Carrier oils are used to dilute essential and other oils before application. They carry the essential oil onto the skin.

In natural skin care, carrier oils are typically referred to as vegetable oils, fixed oils, or base oils.

Carrier oils can contain fat-soluble vitamins, minerals, and other nutrients.

Carrier oils contain Vitamin E, which acts as anti-oxidants. Vitamin E helps extend the shelf life of the carrier oil.

Carrier oils contain Essential Fatty Acids.

EFA are fatty acids that our bodies cannot manufacture and need to get from our diets.

Carrier when applied topically, are very nourishing to our skin.

Each carrier oil offers a different combination of therapeutic properties and characteristics. The choice of carrier oil can depend on the therapeutic benefit being sought.

Natural lotions, creams, body oils, bath oils, lip balms, and other moisturizing skincare products are also made using carrier oils.

ESSENTIAL OIL vs CARRIER OIL

Essential oils are distilled from the leaves, bark, roots, and other aromatic portions of plant material. Essential oils evaporate and have a concentrated aroma.

Carrier oils, on the other hand, are pressed from the fatty portions (seeds, nuts, kernels) and do not evaporate or impart their aroma as strongly as essential oils.

Carrier oils can go rancid over time, but essential oils do not. Instead, essential oils "oxidize" and lose their therapeutic benefits, but they don't go rancid.

The term carrier oil is generally limited to use within the practice of aromatherapy.

In natural skin care, carrier oils are typically referred to as vegetable oils, fixed oils, or base oils.

Some carrier oils are odorless, but generally speaking, most have a faintly sweet, nutty aroma.

ESSENTIAL FATTY ACIDS

The human body can manufacture most fatty acids that we need for optimal health.

Those fatty acids that we cannot manufacture and need to acquire from our diet are called Essential Fatty Acids (EFAs).

Essential Fatty Acids are necessary for human functions and healthy, youthful skin.

Those that are lacking in the proper intake of Essential Fatty Acids may demonstrate seriously dry skin or they may be prone to more serious skin conditions including psoriasis and eczema.

Using carrier oils that are rich in essential fatty acids and including a diet rich in Essential Fatty Acids can significantly help nourish and improve the look and feel of the skin.

Essential Fatty Acids are generally organized into two groups:

Omega-3 Essential Fatty Acids and Omega-6 Essential Fatty Acids.

The hardest to acquire EFAs are the Omega-3 group.

Omega-3 Essential Fatty Acids: Alpha-linolenic acid is the primary Omega-3 Essential Fatty Acid found in plants.

Omega-6 Essential Fatty Acids: Gamma-linolenic acid (GLA) and linoleic acid are examples of Omega-6 Essential Fatty Acids found in plant oils.

CHAPTER EIGHTY-SEVEN

ALMOND CARRIER OIL

Viscosity: Medium.

Absorption: Semi-quickly.

It has a rich concentration of oleic and linoleic essential fatty acids,

It is also nourishing to the skin and well suited for massage.

Sweet almond oil is obtained from the dried kernels of the almond tree and it is an excellent emollient (softening and soothing to the skin) and also helps the skin to balance its loss and absorption of moisture.

It provides a nice "slip and slide" effect without wasting any of the oil.

Sweet almond oil is suitable for all skin types.

Sweet almond oil helps relieve irritation, inflammation, and itching also helps to relieve muscular aches and pains.

Good moisturizer suitable for all skin types helps relieve irritation, inflammation, and itching, and is greatly lubricating and because it is not an overly fast penetrating oil, it is a good massage oil.

Almond oil act as an emollient, skin soother, and softener while conditioning the skin and promoting a clear young-looking complexion, also helps to relieve muscular aches and pains.

Sweet almond oil is one of the most popular carrier oils, since it is non-greasy, spreads easily, and also is good for nourishing the skin.

CHAPTER EIGHTY-EIGHT

APRICOT CARRIER OIL

Viscosity: Medium.

Absorption: Quick

It comes from the kernel of the apricot pit.

Apricot oil is lightweight and easily absorbed by the skin, making it an excellent natural moisturizer. It helps hydrate the skin without leaving a greasy residue, making it suitable for all skin types, including sensitive and oily skin.

Apricot oil glides smoothly over the skin, helping to reduce friction during massage while nourishing and hydrating the skin. Apricot oil is good for facial massage.

Apricot oil can be used as a natural conditioner to moisturize and soften the hair. It helps to hydrate dry, brittle hair, reduce frizz, and add shine.

Apricot oil is effective at removing makeup, including waterproof mascara and long-lasting foundation. Its gentle yet effective cleansing properties help dissolve makeup, dirt, and impurities without stripping the skin of its natural oils. Simply apply apricot oil to a cotton pad and gently wipe away makeup.

Apricot oil can be used to soften and moisturize dry, brittle cuticles, helping to prevent hangnails and promote healthy nail growth. Simply massage a small amount of apricot oil into the cuticles and nails before bedtime.

Apricot oil contains anti-inflammatory compounds such as oleic acid and linoleic acid, which can help soothe irritated or inflamed skin conditions like eczema, psoriasis, and dermatitis.

CHAPTER EIGHTY-NINE

AVOCADO CARRIER OIL

Viscosity: High

Absorption: Semi-quickly.

Avocado oil is one of the carrier oils that are well suited for dry skin and related conditions.

Avocado oil contains lots of vitamins which nourish the skin.

Avocado oilis very rich but it easily combines with other carrier oils.

Avocado oil is a rich heavy oil, that is deeply penetrating and rich in vitamins A, D and E and OMEGA - 3 fatty acids, lecithin, potassium, chlorophyll as well as vitamin E.

Avocado oil is very useful when treating sun or climate damaged skin.

Avocado oil can help moisturize and nourish the hair and scalp.

Avocado can help relax muscles, hydrate the skin, and promote a sense of well-being during massage therapy.

CHAPTER NINETY

ARGAN CARRIER OIL

Viscosity: Medium.

Absorption: Semi-quickly.

Argan oil is pressed from the nut of the fruit from the argan tree, which is found in Morocco.

Argan oil is primarily comprised of fatty acids and a variety of phenolic compounds.

The majority of the fat content of argan oil comes from oleic and linoleic acid

Approximately 29–36% of the fatty acid content of argan oil comes from linoleic acid, or omega-6, making it a good source of this essential nutrient

Additionally, argan oil is a rich source of vitamin E, which is required for healthy skin, hair and eyes. This vitamin also has powerful antioxidant properties

Argan oil removes scars

Argan oil improves nail growth.

Argan oil is often used as a key ingredient in shampoos due to its ability to restore softness, strength, and shine to hair.

Argan oil is gentle, and safe to use around your eyes.

Argan oil has antioxidant and anti-Inflammatory Properties

Argan oil seals in moisture, making hair more manageable and less prone to breakage from brushing and styling.

Argan oil is a good hair and scalp moisturizer

Argan oil is a good lip moisturizer

CHAPTER NINETY-ONE

CASTOR CARRIER OIL

Viscosity: Very High

Absorption: Slow

Castor oil is a thick oil and a cooling oil

Castor oil a natural moisturizer

Castor oil is rich in ricinoleic acid, a monounsaturated fatty acid. These types of fats act as humectants.

Humectants retain moisture by preventing water loss through the outer layer of the skin.

Castor oil is often used in cosmetics to promote hydration and is often added to products like lotions, makeup, and cleansers.

Castor oil promotes wound healing

Castor oil stimulates tissue growth

Castor oil also reduces dryness and cornification

Castor oil has impressive anti-inflammatory effects

Castor oil can reduce acne

Castor oil is anti-fungal

Castor oil can keep your hair and scalp healthy

CHAPTER NINETY-TWO

COCONUT CARRIER OIL

Viscosity: Medium.

Absorption: Semi-quickly.

Coconut oil one of the carrier oils that solidifies at room temperature.

Coconut oil is highest in saturated fats of all the carrier oils used in natural skin care products, twice as saturated as lard.

Coconut oil protects your skin from UV rays.

Coconut oil relieve skin irritation and eczema

Coconut oil moisturize skin

Coconut oil has antibacterial properties

Coconut oil may help reduce belly fat

Coconut oil can help keep your hair healthy.

Coconut oil improves wound healing.

Coconut oil boosts bone health

Coconut oil combat candida.

Coconut oil heal ragged cuticles.

Coconut oil relieve symptoms of arthritis

Coconut oil soothe chapped lips

CHAPTER NINETY-THREE

EPO(EVENING PRIMROSE OIL) CARRIER OIL

Viscosity: Medium.

Absorption: Semi-quickly.

EPO is a fine textured oil and has moisturizing properties.

EPO is found useful to treat eczema, psoriasis, pre-menstrual syndrome (PMS) rheumatoid arthritis as well as weight reduction.

EPO is understood to reduce hyperactivity in babies and young children when rubbed onto their skin.

EPO is often used for conditions affecting women's health, such as breast pain associated with the menstrual cycle, menopausal symptoms, and premenstrual syndrome.

EPO is one of the richest, sources of Gamma-Linolenic acid as it contains about 72% Linoleic acid and 9 percent GLA.

EPO is an anti-oxidant in that it also counter acts the formation of free radicals.

EPO is often used for conditions affecting women's health, such as breast pain associated with the menstrual cycle, menopausal symptoms, and premenstrual syndrome.

EPO may interfere with medications used to treat epilepsy and should be avoided by people taking anti epileptic drugs.

Menopause - Evening primrose oil is often used for conditions affecting women's health, such as breast pain associated with the menstrual cycle, menopausal symptoms, and premenstrual syndrome. PMS suffers were given evening primrose oil three times daily, 67% of the participants were symptom-free and 23% achieved partial relief.

FLAXSEED CARRIER OIL

Viscosity: Medium.

Absorption: Semi-quickly.

Flax Seed Oil contains omega-6 and omega-9 essential fatty acids, B vitamins, potassium, lecithin, magnesium, fiber, protein, and zinc nearly every system in the body can benefit from flaxseed oil natural properties.

Research shows a low incidence of breast cancer and colon cancer in populations that have high amounts of lignan in their diet.

Flax is 100 times richer in lignan than most whole grains.

Shortens recovery time for fatigued muscles after exertion.

Increases the body's production of energy and also increases stamina.

Accelerates the healing of sprains and bruises.

Stimulates brown fat cells and increases the metabolic rate making it easier to burn off fat.

Improves the absorption of Calcium.

Strengthens finger and toenails.

Helpful in the treatment of eczema, psoriasis, and dandruff.

Has been scientifically proven to treat some cases of depression.

Flax Seed oil can help restore the body's natural balance of good and bad prostaglandins.

Flaxseed oil takes a bit of time to be absorbed into the body before the full beneficial effects begin, ranging anywhere from a few days to as many as six weeks, depending on your overall well-being.

CHAPTER NINETY-FIVE

GRAPESEED CARRIER OIL

Viscosity: Medium.

Absorption: Semi-quickly.

Grapeseed oil has a light texture, is mildly astringent, and is often used for acne and oily skin.

Grapeseed oil has mildly astringent qualities which help to tighten and tone the skin, which makes it useful for acne and other skin complaints.

Grapeseed oil is rich in linoleic acid, an essential fatty acid quite important for the skin and the cell membranes.

Grapeseed oil is easily absorbed by the skin.

Grapeseed oil has mildly astringent qualities which help to tighten and tone the skin, which makes it useful for acne and other skin complaints.

Grapeseed oil is rich in linoleic acid, an essential fatty acid quite important for the skin and the cell membranes.

Grapeseed oil has regenerative and restructuring virtues and has great skin moisturizing properties.

Grapeseed oil is a good non-greasy oil to use.

CHAPTER NINETY-SIX

HAZELNUT CARRIER OIL

Viscosity: Medium.

Absorption: Semi-quickly.

Hazelnut oil is one of the most useful carrier oils for facial blends and those with a tendency of having oily skin.

Hazelnut oil is light and mildly fragranced and is easily absorbed into the skin.

Hazelnut oil is one of the best carrier oils for all natural skin care products, including massage oils.

Hazelnut oil, is highly penetrative and is fine textured oil that helps to tone and tighten the skin while strengthening capillaries and assisting in cell regeneration.

Hazelnut oil has good moisturizing qualities

Hazelnut oil is lightweight and easily absorbed by the skin, making it an excellent moisturizer for all skin types, including oily and acne-prone skin.

Hazelnut oil has a light texture and glides smoothly over the skin, making it an ideal carrier oil for massage therapy.

Hazelnut oil helps to hydrate the skin without clogging pores and can be used alone or blended with other skincare oils.

Hazelnut oil can be used as a natural conditioner to moisturize and nourish the hair and scalp. It helps to soften and detangle hair, reduce frizz, and add shine.

CHAPTER NINETY-SEVEN

JOJOBA CARRIER OIL

Viscosity: Medium.

Absorption: Good

Shelf Life: Very Stable.

Jojoba oil is one of the most common carrier oils for use in natural skincare products. It is technically not oil but a liquid wax derived from the seed of the desert shrub. It will not oxidize or become rancid and as such is often used to extend the shelf life of natural skincare products.

Jojoba oil is very similar to the sebum produced by our skin and so is particularly beneficial in facial and body oils.

Jojoba oil is also useful for this same reason in scalp and hair treatments.

Jojoba oil is composed of wax esters, it is an extremely stable substance and does not easily deteriorate and the structure closely resembles that of your skin sebum, making it an excellent moisturizer and ideal for all skin types.

When jojoba oil used as a massage medium, it acts as an emulsifier with the skin's natural sebum and gently unclogs the pores, and lifts grime and embedded impurities.

Jojoba oil contains myristic acid which also has anti-inflammatory actions and since it has a similar composition to that of the skin's oils, it is quickly absorbed and is excellent for dry and mature skins as well as inflamed conditions.

Jojoba oil is a good nourishing ingredient for hair care

Jojoba oil can be used on acne skin as it helps to control acne, it is also an antioxidant.

CHAPTER NINETY-EIGHT

MACADAMIA CARRIER OIL

Viscosity: Medium.

Absorption: Semi-quickly.

Macadamia oil contains high amounts of palmitoleic acid, which is also normally found in the sebum of man, and this oil, therefore, has a great affinity to our skin

Macadamia oil is very emollient and is therefore great for dry and aging skin.

Macadamia oil is good to use where sebum production has reduced.

Macadamia oil has good emollient properties and for this reason, is good to include in any base massage oil blend.

Macadamia oil is readily absorbed and helps to soften the skin and is also said to help reduce fine lines when used in facial massage.

Macadamia oil is deeply moisturizing and helps to nourish and protect the skin from environmental damage.

Macadamia oil can be used as a standalone moisturizer or added to creams, lotions, and serums.

Macadamia oil is lightweight and easily absorbed by the hair and scalp, making it an excellent choice for hair care products.

Macadamia oil helps to hydrate and nourish the hair, leaving it soft, smooth, and shiny.

Macadamia oil has a smooth texture and glides easily over the skin, making it ideal for use as a massage oil.

Macadamia oil contains anti-inflammatory compounds that can help soothe and calm irritated skin conditions such as eczema, psoriasis, and dermatitis.

CHAPTER NINETY-NINE

NEEM CARRIER OIL

Viscosity: Very High

Absorption: Slow

Neem oil should only be used externally on the skin and has been therapeutically used as folk medicine to control respiratory disorders, constipation, leprosy, as well as a general tonic.

Neem has been used for the topical treatment of rheumatism, eczema, ringworm, athlete's foot, cold sores, psoriasis, warts, chronic syphilitic sores, infected burn wounds, and slow-healing skin ulcers as well as controlling various skin infections.

Neem has anti-inflammatory, antipyretic, and analgesic, activity and possesses immunostimulant activity.

Neem is highly effective against human fungi, including trichophyton, epidermophyton, microsporum, trichosporon, geotricum, and candida.

Neem is effective against a wide spectrum of bacteria.

Neem can kill head lice.

Neem is a mosquito repellant.

Neem can be used to protect plants.

Neem can be used to protect pets from ticks and fleas.

Taking Neem oil internally is not recommended.

OLIVE CARRIER OIL

Viscosity: Medium.

Absorption: Semi-quickly.

Olive oil is good for healthy hair, skin, and nails.

Olive oil is good for dry skin.

Olive oil contains between 60 and 80% of monounsaturated fats (in this case, oleic acid), which help to reduce "bad cholesterol" (LDL) and preserve "good cholesterol" (HDL).

Olive oil contains vitamin E and polyphenols that are known as antioxidants that suppress the free radicals and oxidization process.

Olive oil has vitamins A, D, K, and especially E.

Olive oil has just the right amount of linoleic acid, which is essential for the human diet, although in excess it can cause oxidation, which is harmful to our health.

Olive oil also helps to maintain low blood pressure and to alleviate arthritis.

Vitamin E in Olive oil is fat-soluble, which means it can be stored in the body.

Olive oil as an anti-inflammatory

Olive oil aids digestion and helps the body to absorb calcium.

Olive oil helps to improve the appearance and texture of our skin.

The properties of Extra Virgin olive oil are very similar to that of your skin so it is used in lip balm, shampoo, bath oils, hand lotions, soap, soak for nails, massage oil, dandruff treatment, etc.

Extra Virgin Olive Oil - Virgin olive oil whose free acidity, expressed as oleic acid, is not more than 1 gram per 100 grams.

PUMPKINSEED CARRIER OIL

Viscosity: Medium.

Absorption: Semi-quickly.

The pumpkin seed oil has good healing qualities for skin problems such as sores and ulcers.

Pumpkin seed oil helps you get smooth skin.

Pumpkin seed oil reduces Inflammation

Pumpkin seed oil aids in joint lubrication and reducing the pain and discomfort associated with arthritis.

Pumpkin seed oil boosts antioxidant properties.

Pumpkin seed oil stimulates the growth of new cells,

Pumpkin seed oil defends against infections and oxidative stress in skin cells.

Pumpkin seed oil reduces the appearance of wrinkles and blemishes related to age.

Pumpkin seed oil is also a rich source of vitamin E, which has powerful effects on skin appearance and texture.

Pumpkin seed oil helps stimulate circulation by eliminating sluggish blood.

Pumpkin seed oil Increases bone strength.

ROSEHIP CARRIER OIL

Viscosity: Medium.

Absorption: Semi-quickly.

Rosehip oil contains beta-carotene, vitamins A, C & E, and fatty acids omega 3, 6 and 9.

Rosehip oil is a powerful moisturizer.

Use rosehip oil in the evening to boost your skin's ability to heal overnight.

Use rosehip oil as a night-time moisturizer instead of a heavy night cream.

Apply Rosehip Oil for cracked or splitting cuticles and over fingernails to strengthen them.

Use rosehip oil for your eyes to diminish fine lines.

Rosehip oil massage onto pregnant bellies to prevent stretch marks.

Rosehip Oil massage all over face, neck and décolletage to reverse the affects of photo aging

Use rosehip oil on legs, arms, underarm areas and more after shaving to give smoother skin.

Apply rosehip oil to your scalp and pull through your hair and leave on for 30 minutes or so before showering to give added bounce and moisture.

Apply rosehip oil daily after cleansing to acne-prone skin to treat acne scarring and prevent future breakouts.

Apply rosehip oil to knees, elbows, cracked heels, and other rough skin to soften roughness.

SESAME CARRIER OIL

Viscosity: High

Absorption: Semi-quickly.

Sesame seed oil has long been used in Ayurvedic medicinal preparations and is said to be rejuvenating.

Sesame seed oil is a good source of vitamins E and B complex and minerals such as calcium, magnesium and phosphorus.

Sesame seed oil further contains protein as well as lecithin.

Sesame seed oil is a thick oil it is used for eczema, psoriasis as well as older and mature skin and it contains excellent moisturizing properties.

Sesame seed oil massage oil has good moisturizing, soothing and emollient qualities which makes it a good choice to include when mixing a massage oil or preparing a carrier oil blend.

Sesame seed oil is a good source of vitamins and minerals we find it to be a good oil to use in a blend when preparing a massage base oil.

WALNUT CARRIER OIL

Viscocity: High

Absorption: Dries quickly

Walnut oil contains useful amounts of essential fatty acids including linoleic acid.

Walnut oil is highly penetrative and is fine textured and is one of the most highly unsaturated vegetable oils.

Walnut oil makes a great carrier oil blend for the purpose of massaging the body.

Walnut oil is known for its soothing refreshing emollient qualities.

Walnut oil is a preferred oil owing to its therapeutic properties.

Walnut oil is extremely useful in combating skin problems.

Walnut oil is an oil that helps to tone and tighten the skin while strengthening capillaries and assisting in cell regeneration

Walnut massage oil has great moisturizing qualities which makes it a good choice to include when mixing a massage oil or preparing a carrier oil blend.

Walnut oil has good astringent qualities, which makes it a good carrier oil to use on oily and combination skins

WHEATGERM CARRIER OIL

Viscocity: High

Absorption: Slow

Wheatgerm oil is very high in vitamin E and essential fatty acids

Wheatgerm oil is dark in appearance and has a strong odor.

Wheatgerm oil is often added to other carrier oils to help lengthen their shelf life.

Wheatgerm oil is rich in vitamin A, vitamin B, vitamin D, vitamin B1, vitamin B2, vitamin B3, and vitamin B6. The other ingredients are potassium, zinc, sulphur, phosphorous, and iron.

Wheatgerm oil when applied topically to the skin it helps promote the formation of new cells improves circulation, and to helps repair sun damage to the skin.

Wheatgerm oil is also used to help relieve the symptoms of dermatitis.

Wheatgerm oil's anti-oxidant property allows it to mix well with other essential and carrier oils.

Wheatgerm oil also used as an emollient

Wheatgerm oil improves blood circulation

Wheatgerm oil repairs damaged skin cells.

Wheatgerm oil softens dry skin.

Wheatgerm oil you to get rid of scars.

Wheatgerm oil helps in the treatment of aging skin.

Wheatgerm oil helps in the treatment of eczerma.

Wheatgerm oil helps in lymph and muscle function.

Wheatgerm oil helps to heal wounds.

Wheatgerm oil should not be exposed to high temperatures as its quality gets degraded.

www.ingramcontent.com/pod-product-compliance
Lightning Source LLC
Chambersburg PA
CBHW051240130726
47988CB00001B/430